Physical Security

Principles of Physical Security

Library of Congress
Catalog Card Number:
77-86192

ISBN: 0-87201-748-6

Contents

I wish to acknowledge the assistance of a good friend, and an expert in the field of private security, Mr. Larry Wark, President of Aries International Inc., Fort Lauderdale, Florida. His contribution and encouragement were vital to the completion of this text.

to "Dusty"

Introduction

Physical Security

Physical security is the physical measures designed to safeguard personnel, to prevent unauthorized access to material (equipment, facilities, and documents), and to protect it against sabotage, damage, and theft.

This definition must be interpreted and applied in its fullest and broadest sense. Physical security cannot be viewed as merely an "interior guard" function to be performed at a fixed installation. It is, in fact, an active and aggressive function with many facets, ranging from fixed-post security to actual operations. Physical security must, above all, be thoroughly and continually studied, in all areas and operations; and physical security safeguard measures should be thoroughly planned, continually reviewed, and aggressively implemented. Physical security must also be understood to apply to internal control procedures of all types.

Perfect or absolute security is always the goal of those responsible for the security of an installation or activity; but such a state of absolute security can never be fully attained. There is no object so well protected that it cannot be stolen, damaged, destroyed, or observed by unauthorized eyes. The purpose of physical security, then, is (a) to make access so difficult (provide measurable delay time) that an intruder will hesitate to attempt penetration, or (b) to provide for his apprehension should he be successful. Security must be built upon a system of defense in depth, or accumulated delay time.

Physical security is only part of the overall defense of an installation. It does not include dispersion of facilities or continuity of operations.

It is not economically possible or theoretically necessary that installations and activities of every kind and character achieve the same degree of protection. The degree of protection warranted in any particular installation is predicated upon an analysis of two factors: criticality and

1

vulnerability. If the installation is both highly critical and highly vulnerable, then an extensive physical security program is a necessity. Because of the cost of physical protective measures (in terms of money and manpower), many security forces will not be able to achieve maximum protection for the entire installation or activity. Therefore, the specific criticality and vulnerability of the various areas must be determined, and available resources apportioned accordingly. Special protection is thus provided for the most critical and vulnerable areas, while areas of lesser importance and susceptibility are given a smaller degree of protection.

The critical portion of an installation or activity is one in which partial or complete loss would have an immediate and serious impact on the ability of the installation or activity to perform its function for a considerable period of time. The relative criticality of such portion may have no direct relationship to size or whether it produces an end product; this must be determined on the basis of its importance to the installation or activity as a whole.

Vulnerability is a function of the hazards which could cause sufficient loss, damage, or destruction to affect the operation of the area or installation under consideration. If one or more hazards exist which could easily achieve this result, the relative vulnerability is high. As it becomes more unlikely that existing hazards may interfere with the mission, vulnerability becomes lower.

Factors Influencing Physical Security Requirements

Factors affecting the degree and type of physical security required for an installation or activity area are its size, the nature and sensitivity of its mission, vulnerability of equipment, geographic location, the economic and political situation of the area, the proximity of external support, and the capabilities of potential intruders. The factors affecting the degree and type of physical security required for *property* at an installation or activity are its vulnerability to theft or damage, attractiveness as an object of sabotage or theft, monetary value, and availability of like installations or substitute facilities.

The scope of the physical security program employed in any installation or activity should be the result of an evaluation of the following criteria:

1. Criticality;
2. Vulnerability to potential hazards, damage, or loss;
3. Effect of physical security measures on efficiency and operations;
4. Practical limitations imposed by the physical characteristics of the installation or activity;
5. Availability of funds;

6. Alternate measures or techniques;
7. Evaluation and appraisal of the physical security capabilities of all available resources.

Security management must continually evaluate its installation's position in terms of these factors and devise physical security measures accordingly.

Security Hazards

Security hazards may be present constantly or they may exist at infrequent and unpredictable intervals. The mere possibility of their existence constitutes a security risk. The degree of risk involved depends on two factors:

1. The probability of adverse effects occurring as a direct result of the hazard;
2. The extent to which the installation or activity will be affected by such hazard.

Because many security hazards are also safety hazards, the physical security program must be closely coordinated with the safety program.

Security Hazards Defined

Security hazards are acts or conditions which may result in the compromise of information; loss of life; damage, loss, or destruction of property; or disruption of the mission of the installation or facility. Before the physical security officer can develop an effective security program, he must determine the possibility of interference with the operational capabilities of the installation or facility from any and all sources. Recognition of all risks is essential if he is to make recommendations for physical security measures to control or eliminate them. The severity of security hazards will depend on such variables as the type of installation or facility involved, mission or processes performed, physical layout, and construction. The geographical location and the existing state of law and order are also critical factors.

Security hazards are categorized into two types: natural and manmade.

Natural hazards are usually the consequence of natural phenomena, though some can be induced by human action. Although natural hazards usually cannot be prevented, it is essential to remember that they will greatly affect security operations. Protective measures must be increased since natural hazards may reduce the effectiveness of security measures already in effect: perimeter fences may be down, protective lights and alarm systems may not operate, patrol vehicles may be damaged beyond utilization, and property may be scattered over a large area for easy access to any one who desires to take it. Any one or a combination of these effects will require immediate reinforcement of the security force and implementation of additional physical protection measures to meet emergency and disaster requirements. Again, physical security plans must be closely coordinated with installation emergency and disaster plans. Examples of natural hazards are:

1. Floods—flooding of the installation with resulting property damage, destruction of perimeter barriers, and short-circuiting of alarm devices. Heavy rains or snowfalls, even though they do not result in floods, may cause some of the same damages.

2. Storms—high winds or rain causing alarm devices to short-circuit, causing nuisance alarms, and limiting visibility.

3. Earthquakes—causing nuisance alarms, possible fires from broken gas mains, buildings weakening and falling down.

4. Winds—disrupting power lines, setting off nuisance alarms, causing hazards with flying debris.

5. Snow and ice—blocking patrol roads, increasing response time to alarms, and the freezing of locks and alarm mechanisms.

6. Fires—damage/destruction of natural and physical perimeter barriers or buildings.

For planning and implementing effective security measures against natural hazards, see Chapters 3, 5, 7 and 9.

Man-made hazards involve the result of a state of mind, attitude, weakness, or other traits of one or more persons. They include acts of commission on the operation or mission of an installation or facility. Security planning must be based on the assumption that a risk does exist from such hazards. Examples are:

1. Industrial accidents—explosions and fires;

2. Civil disturbances—riots and other acts of civil disobedience that may threaten the security of the installation or facility;

3. Sabotage—incendiarism, explosives, and mechanical or contamination sabotage;

4. Pilferage;

5. Carelessness and accidents can disrupt operations, destroy critical materiel, and inflict casualties among personnel. Both of these hazards normally result either directly or indirectly from acts or omissions by employees in performance of their duties. Therefore, supervisory and management personnel have the primary responsibility for control of these hazards. But security forces must be alert to observe, report, and take emergency actions to correct potentially dangerous conditions. Security

personnel can make valuable contributions to the safety program in both the planning and application phases.

Sabotage

Recognizing sabotage is often difficult, as the ultimate target may not be readily apparent and the act itself frequently destroys evidence of sabotage. Effective countermeasures against the threat of sabotage begin with understanding some of the methods and targets of the saboteur. This section discusses the methods of accomplishing the principal types of sabotage and the saboteur's probable targets. It is not intended to be a complete text on the subject, for the saboteur is limited only by his imagination and ingenuity.

Sabotage as Diversion. Sabotage, particularly in the form of fire or minor explosions, may also be used as a diversion to permit pilferage, by drawing attention to the affected area and away from the object of the pilferage. This hazard exists particularly when security personnel are also responsible for fire fighting and similar control operations.

Saboteurs and Their Methods

A saboteur may be a highly trained professional or a rank amateur. He may be a laborer, a machinist, a foreman, a top-flight engineer, or even a member of management. He may be anyone. But one thing is certain: he is likely to be one of the least suspected members of the organization. Saboteurs may work alone or in groups. They may infiltrate industrial groups as legitimate members, or they may work from the outside. Characteristics of a typical independent saboteur are:

1. No affiliation with foreign or military group
2. Discontented employee
3. Very vulnerable to subversive propaganda
4. May be mentally ill
5. Actions cannot be predicted or anticipated
6. Acts on impulse
7. No special training for sabotage

There are many ways to commit sabotage, and new methods and devices are constantly being adopted. A major sabotage effort may be undertaken after thorough study of the physical layout of the facility and its production processes by technical personnel fully qualified to select the most effective method to strike one or more of the most vulnerable parts of the facility. On the other hand, the saboteur may rely solely upon his own knowledge of the facility and the materials available to him. The device or agent selected for sabotage may range from the crude or elementary to the ingenious or scientific. The methods of sabotage may be generally classified as follows: fire, explosive devices, mechanical, chemical and psychological.

Fire

The malicious use of fire is one of the oldest methods of sabotage. It is one of the most effective because it can destroy the evidence as well as the objective. By using a timing device, the saboteur can leave the area and establish an alibi, and it is entirely possible that the fire itself will leave minimum identifiable traces of its causes. Personnel assigned fire-fighting duties must be trained in the recognition of the various incendiary materials which may be used, and in the use of the appropriate extinguishing agent. Assistance in such training can be obtained from local fire departments.

Incendiary Materials

Some of the common materials which alone or in combination form incendiary mixtures are:

1. Phosphorous—a waxy, yellowish, translucent solid that burns spontaneously when exposed to air. It is stored in water, in which it is insoluble. Then used to impregnate paper or cloth, it is first dissolved in carbon disulphide. Upon exposure to air the carbon disulphide slowly evaporates, leaving particles of phosphorous which burst into flame. Phosphorous is also used in explosive type incendiaries where detonation scatters the particles over wide areas.

2. Sodium—a metallic element that ignites on contact with water. It is naturally shiny but oxidizes quickly and becomes covered with a brownish patina. It is most effective when combined with other chemicals, and as an incendiary device it is particularly useful in waterfront sabotage.

3. Thermite—a mixture of iron oxide and aluminum powder. It can be molded into various shapes and is used extensively in incendiary bombs. It is best triggered by magnesium tape, and burns with an intense heat.

4. Potassium permanganate—an oxidizing agent which, when combined with glycerin, is spontaneously combustible. By using a capillary tube with a stop clock an effective delayed-action device can readily be made.

Explosives

Sabotage by the use of explosives instantaneously destroys at least part of the area, and the initial damage may be followed by a fire. The most probable targets are the heavy construction of power and transportation facilities. Small quantities of explosives may trigger a chain reaction or destroy an extremely vital portion of an installation. One problem to the saboteur using explosives is the difficulty of surreptitiously bringing the explosive to the facility: no more than approximately three pounds of the above explosives can be concealed on a person. Yet a saboteur may use any ingenious method to accomplish his mission.

Explosives are readily available and are used extensively in mining, agricultural, and some industrial operations. And they are not difficult to produce—the ingredients are readily procurable.

Explosives are classified as low explosives or high explosives according to the time it takes them to burn or detonate. The slower-acting low explosives have a pushing effect, whereas high explosives have a shattering effect.

Low Explosives

1. *Black powder* is the oldest known explosive, but its use has declined due to the development of more efficient types of explosives. It is granular, and the size of the grains varies for different usages. In appearance it is shiny black and in burning gives off a heavy white smoke. It burns freely in the open air and must be confined for an explosive effect. It is used in pipe bombs and other improvised devices.

2. *Smokeless powder* is not a powder and is only smokeless in comparison to black powder. It is made by treating plant fibers (cotton or wood) with nitric and sulphuric acids to form nitrocellulose. It may be used in pipe bombs and similar arrangements in the same manner as black powder, and it generally has a more powerful effect.

High Explosives

1. *Nitroglycerin* is an oily, colorless liquid that explodes violently, but due to its sensitivity to shock, it is not widely used in its liquid state. When combined with other materials, it loses its sensitivity and is made into dynamite and plastic explosives.

2. *Dynamite* is the most widely used commercial explosive. Basically, it is nitroglycerin absorbed in a porous or absorbent material, such as sawdust. The percentage of nitroglycerin varies, and other ingredients are added to fit the intended use. It is packed in sticks, usually round, and covered with paraffin-impregnated paper. The strength is marked on the outside of the wrapper. A blasting cap detonator is necessary to cause an explosion. If dynamite is stored in one position for a long period, however, the nitroglycerin tends to seep to the lower side and becomes sensitive. Its

convenience, availability, and effectiveness make dynamite a favorite explosive for the saboteur. The high velocity of its explosion makes it unnecessary to confine it to make an effective bomb.

3. *Trinitrotoluene* (TNT) is a yellow solid, usually formed into blocks of various sizes. Because of its insensitivity to shock, its ease of handling, and its powerful explosive properties, it is excellent for sabotage purposes.

4. *Nitrostarch* is also an excellent explosive for sabotage for the same reasons as TNT. It is slightly less powerful than TNT, but more sensitive to flame, friction, and impact.

5. Compositions C3 and C4 are yellow and white respectively, and are odorous and plastic. They have about the same sensitivity as TNT but are more powerful.

Handling Bombs

The exterior appearance of a known or suspected bomb gives *little or no indication* of the explosive used or the manner of construction. Both of these key factors are largely dependent upon the availability of materials and the technical skill of the saboteur. In view of the infinite varieties possible, it is obvious that no set procedure can be established for their handling. However, the primary consideration is the safety of life and property, and there are certain basic rules which must be followed. Wherever the possibility of sabotage bomb exists, there must be a prearranged plan for coping with such an emergency so that the following steps may be carried out quickly and in many cases concurrently:

1. Clear the area of all personnel and establish a guard around the danger zone.
2. Send for technical help.
3. IMMEDIATELY notify the security force headquarters.
4. Shut off power, gas and fuel lines leading into the danger area.
5. Notify the fire department.
6. Secure mattresses or sandbags for use as protective shields and barricades. Sandbags may also be used in confining and directing the force of an explosion.
7. Remove flammable materials and small objects from the surrounding area. However, anything that might be connected with the bomb or that might act as a trigger mechanism must not be touched.

Except in an emergency presenting immediate danger to life, inexperienced personnel should not handle or attempt to dispose of any explosive material. Inexperienced personnel should take the above precautionary steps and await the arrival of qualified Explosive Disposal personnel.

Mechanical Sabotage

Mechanical sabotage can be carried out without special knowledge or training, and the necessary means are frequently built into the target. The will to damage or impede is sufficient, whether the motivation is personal or ideological.

The methods of mechanical sabotage are usually within one of the following classifications (however, the field is wide, and they may be used either singly or in combination):

1. *Breakage.* Breakage is usually directed against the moving parts of a machine or motor, or against delicate control or measuring devices. A wrench dropped into the moving parts of a machine, or a broken pressure gauge, will cause a halt to service or production.

2. *Abrasives.* Abrasives, such as emery, sand, powdered glass, or carborundum, introduced directly into the moving parts of a machine or into the fuel or lubricating systems will cause undue wear and eventual breakdown. *Carborundum is an abrasive used in grindstones, i.e. Revolving stone disc to sharpen bladed tools.*

3. *Contamination.* Contamination of the fuel of an internal combustion engine is one of the most common methods of mechanical sabotage. Ordinary granulated sugar poured into a gasoline tank will immobilize a motor and necessitate overhaul.

4. *Substitution.* Items such as raw materials, processing solutions, measuring gauges, patterns or blueprints may be altered by substituting faulty materials or erroneous information.

5. *Acts of omission.* An act of omission is the failure to do something which it is a duty to do. Deliberate failure to lubricate moving parts of a machine, causing it to break down, is an act of omission and sabotage.

The infinite variety and the simplicity of methods for committing an act of mechanical sabotage make it extremely difficult to detect or prevent. Constant vigilance, alert supervision, and frequent inspection by all concerned are the most effective defenses.

Pilferage

Pilferage is probably the most common and annoying hazard with which security personnel will be concerned. It can become such a financial menace and detriment to operations that a large portion of the security guard force may have to be devoted to its control. Pilferage, particularly petty pilferage, is frequently difficult to detect, hard to prove, and dangerous to ignore. *(see p. 116)*

For an exhaustive discussion of methods for controlling pilferage and for evaluating the adequacy of your physical security program in this regard, see Chapter 8.

Unfortunately, determining the amount of loss which may be occurring is not always an easy task. Accounting methods may not be designed to pinpoint thefts; consequently such losses remain undisclosed or are lumped together with other shrinkages, effectively camouflaging them. One of the most common inventory methods is to conduct periodic inventories of property and assume that unaccounted-for inventory loss is due to theft. This is a convenient but deceptive and dangerous method because theft is only one of many causes for inventory shrinkage. Failure to detect shortages in incoming shipments, improper stock usage, poor stock accounting, poor warehousing, improper handling and recording of defective and damaged stock, and resulting inaccurate inventories will cause inventory losses which may be inaccurately labeled as pilferage.

In some cases inventory losses may be impossible to detect because of the nature and quantities of materials involved. Stock inventory records may not be locally maintained, or there may be no method for spot checks or running inventories for discovering shortages. This situation should be corrected where possible—recommend that running inventories be maintained.

An established estimate of the severity of this hazard may have to be revised because of anticipated changes in the economic or social conditions in nearby communities, increases in numbers of employees, introduction of new materials into the installation, or any of the other variables on which estimates of expected losses are based. In any case, the degree of risk involved can be determined only by analysis of the relative vulnerability to pilferage of each area or activity of the installation. To do this, it is necessary to consider who is likely to steal and what items they are most likely to take.

Types of Pilferers

There are two types of pilferers which physical security personnel must be prepared to counteract—or at least recognize—so that proper physical security measures may be taken. These are casual pilferers and systematic pilferers.

A *casual pilferer* is one who steals primarily because he is unable to resist the temptation of an unexpected opportunity and has little fear of detection. There is usually little or no planning or premeditation involved in casual pilferage, and he normally acts alone. He may take items for which he has no immediate need or foreseeable use, or he may take small quantities of supplies for use of family or friends. The degree of risk involved in casual pilferage is normally slight unless many persons are involved. Casual pilferage will occur whenever the individual feels the need or desire for a certain article and poor security measures provide the opportunity to take it. Though it involves unsystematic theft of small articles, casual pilferage is nevertheless very serious, and it may have a great cumulative effect if permitted to become widespread—especially if the stolen items have a high cash or potential value. There is always the possibility that casual pilferers, encouraged by successful theft, may turn to systematic pilferage. Casual pilferers are normally employees and usually are the most difficult to detect and apprehend.

A *systematic pilferer* is one who steals according to preconceived plans, and who steals any and all types of supplies for the purpose of selling them for cash or bartering them for other valuable or desirable commodities. He may work with another person or with a well-organized group of people, some of whom may even be in an advantageous position to locate or administratively control desired items, or remove them from storage areas or transit facilities. Pilferage may be a one-time occurrence or it may extend over a period of months, or even years.

Large quantities of supplies, with great value, may be lost to groups of persons engaged in elaborately planned and carefully executed systematic pilferage activities. Systematic pilferers may or may not be employees of the installation; if they are not, they frequently operate in conspiracy with such employees.

Opportunities for Pilferage

Pilferage may occur anywhere. Even supplies which are stationary in permanent or semi-permanent storage areas or warehouses are vulnerable to theft if adequate precautionary measures are not taken; and vulnerability increases as supplies become more mobile. New and greater opportunities for pilferage are present when supplies are being transported in trucks, trains, planes or ships. The greatest vulnerability and the widest variety of opportunities occur at the various points where supplies are transferred from one means of transportation to another, or from storage to transportation and vice versa. Anyone may be a pilferer. Where need or desire exists, and opportunity is presented, theft is almost a certainty.

Pilferage Targets

Both the casual and systematic pilferer have certain problems to overcome in accomplishing their objectives:

1. The pilferer's first problem is to locate the item or items to be stolen. For the casual pilferer this may be accomplished through individual search or even accidental discovery. In systematic pilferage, more extensive means are generally employed. These may be surveillance by members of the group or the checking of shipping and storage areas or documents by those who have access to them.

2. Next the pilferer must have access to the desired items and gain possession of them. This may involve something as simple as breaking open a box; or it may be as complex as surveying weaknesses in such security factors as physical safeguards or security procedures, attempting to bribe security forces, altering or forging shipping documents or passes, or creating disturbances to divert the attention of security personnel while the actual theft is taking place.

3. The third problem is removing the stolen items to a place where the thief may benefit from his act. Stolen articles of clothing may be worn; small items may be concealed in any of many possible places on the body of the thief or in his vehicle(s); and, through falsification of documents, whole truckloads of supplies may be removed from their proper place without immediate discovery.

4. Finally, to derive any benefit from his act, the pilferer must use the item himself or dispose of it in some way. The casual pilferage of supplies is intended primarily to satisfy the need or desire of the individual thief. The systematic pilferer will usually attempt to sell the material, probably through "fences" or pawnbrokers. The detection of use or disposal offers a chance to prevent further similar pilferage through investigation and discovery of the means used to accomplish the original theft. Similarly, each of the problems faced by would-be pilferers offers opportunities for constructive preventive measures. Careful study of the possible opportunities for the pilferer to solve his problems is essential in security work.

The systematic pilferer's primary concern in selecting a target is its monetary value. This means that he must have or be able to find a ready market for items of property which he may be able to steal. He pilfers small items of relatively high value such as drugs, valuable metals, or electronic items, including radio and television tubes. However, we cannot discount the possibility that a systematic pilferer may, if the profit is substantial, select a target which is of great size and weight. As a general rule, bulk storage areas contain most of the material which may be selected by systematic pilferers.

The casual pilferer is likely to take any item which is easily accessible to him. Since he normally will remove the item from the installation by concealing it on his person or in his automobile, size is also the important consideration. Monetary value and available markets are not of any great concern to the casual pilferer, because he usually has no thought of selling the property he steals. Any property which is not secured or under surveillance, and which is small enough to be hidden on the person or otherwise removed from the installation by commonly available means, is subject to casual pilferage. Storage areas containing loose items are more likely to tempt casual pilferers than are bulk storage areas.

Methods of Pilferage

There are many ways by which pilfered items may be removed. Because the motives and targets of systematic and casual pilferers are very different, the methods of operation for each will likewise be dissimilar. As stated above, the casual pilferer will steal whatever is available to him and generally will remove it from the installation by concealing it on his person or in his automobile. The methods of the systematic pilferer are much more varied and complex. The means which he may employ are limited only by his ingenuity. The following are cited as examples:

1. Shipping and receiving operations are extremely vulnerable to systematic pilferage. It is here that installation personnel and truck drivers have direct contact with each other and a readily available means of conveyance, which offers a tempting opportunity for collusion. Although most truck drivers and employees are honest, a few may succumb to such temptations as a receiving clerk who will certify the receipt of property which the truck driver actually disposed of prior to his arrival at the installation. An installation employee can provide a truck driver with property and assist in concealing it aboard the truck for unauthorized removal from the installation. Employees can assist a truck driver in removing property by executing a fictitious invoice which may appear to be legitimate when inspected by security personnel.

2. Railway employees assigned to switching duties on the installation can operate in a similar manner but with more difficulty because a railway car normally cannot be directed to a desired location so that stolen property can be removed. Additional confederates will usually be required to transfer the stolen goods from the railway car, at some point or siding outside the installation, into some other means of transportation for removal to the ultimate destination. This increase in the number of persons involved will reduce the pilferers' profits and increase the chances for discovery and apprehension.

3. Trash disposal and salvage disposal activities offer excellent opportunities for the systematic pilferer to gain access to valuable material. Property may be hidden in waste material to be recovered by a confederate whose duty is to remove trash from the installation. Serviceable or even new items of equipment or material may be classified as salvage by dishonest employees who are operating in collusion with other persons working in or having access to salvage disposal.

4. Other methods which may be employed by systematic pilferers to remove property include throwing items over fences to be retrieved at a later time by themselves or by confederates; packaging property and sending it to outside addresses through mail channels; collusion with security personnel; loose-fitting clothing that can be worn to conceal small

items; and removal of items on vehicles belonging to outside contractors and vendors.

Measures for Control of Casual Pilferage

Specific measures for prevention of pilferage must be based on careful analysis of the conditions at each installation. The most practical and effective method for controlling casual pilferage is the establishment of psychological deterrents. This may be accomplished in a number of ways:

1. One of the most common means of discouraging casual pilferage is to search individuals and vehicles leaving the installation at unannounced times and places. These "spot searches" may occasionally detect attempts of theft, but their greatest value is in making all employees aware that they may be apprehended if they attempt the illegal removal of property. Care must be taken to insure that personnel are not demoralized nor their legal rights violated by oppressive physical controls or unethical security practices.

2. An aggressive security education program is an effective means of convincing employees that they have much more to lose than gain by stealing. Case histories may be cited where employees were discharged or prosecuted for pilferage. In discussing these cases care must be taken to preclude the identification of individuals, because of possible civil suits for defamation of character and because it is generally poor policy to publicize derogatory information about an individual. It is important for all employees to realize that pilferage is morally wrong no matter how insignificant the value of the item taken.

3. It is particularly important for supervisory personnel to set a proper example and maintain a desirable moral climate for all employees.

4. All employees must be impressed with the fact that they have a responsibility to report any loss to proper authorities.

5. Adequate inventory and control measures should be instituted to account for all material, supplies and equipment. Poor accountability, if its existence is commonly known, is one of the greatest temptations to the casual pilferer. One control method is the requirement for signing for all tools and equipment to be used by individuals. The use of the signature control method reduces the temptation to "pocket" the item.

6. The identification of all tools and equipment by some mark or code, where feasible, is necessary so that property can be identified.

7. In establishing any deterrent to casual pilferage, physical security officers must not lose sight of the fact that most employees are honest and disapprove of thievery. Mutual respect between security personnel and other employees of the installation must be maintained if the facility is to be protected from other more dangerous human hazards. *Any security*

Figure 1. Prevention of pilferage requires alertness and aggressiveness on the part of all security personnel. For critical areas, security surveillance should be established for all exits and entrances to the installation.

measure which infringes on the human rights or dignity of others will jeopardize rather than enhance the overall protection of the installation.

Measures for Control of Systematic Pilferage

Unlike the casual pilferer, the systematic thief will not be discouraged by psychological controls. Nothing short of active physical security measures will be effective in eliminating losses from this source. Some of these would be to:

1. Establish security surveillance of all exits from the installation.
2. Establish an effective package and material control system.
3. Locate parking areas for private vehicles outside the perimeter fencing of the installation.

4. Eliminate potential thieves during the hiring procedure by careful screening and observation.
5. Investigate all losses quickly and efficiently.
6. Establish an effective key control system.
7. Establish adequate security patrols to check buildings, grounds, perimeter, and likely locations which might be used for the clandestine storage of property which has been removed from its proper location.
8. Install mechanical and electrical intrusion detection devices where applicable and practical.
9. Coordinate with supply personnel to establish customer identification as a means to authenticate supply release documents at warehouses and exit gates.
10. Establish appropriate perimeter fencing, lighting, and parking facilities and effective pedestrian, railway, and vehicle gate security controls.
11. Store bulk quantities of highly pilferable stock in enclosed security areas and distribute from there to using section in limited amounts.
12. Establish accurate methods of taking physical inventories and of accounting for stock procurement, usage and salvage.
13. Establish close liaison with appropriate law enforcement agencies.
14. Coordinate closely with supervisors and personnel officers to assure that complete information on offenders is available to them for appropriate action. In some cases, offense reports should be hand-carried.

Prevention

Prevention of pilferage requires alertness and aggressiveness on the part of all security personnel, careful planning and implementation of physical security measures, and an extensive security education program for all employees of the installation. The prevention of pilferage is a continuing process of careful attention. All means available, from the use of informants to the installation of latest devices, must be employed to insure timely information on illegal activities which may lead to serious financial losses.

2

Physical Security Forces

The security force of an installation or facility is the enforcement arm of the physical security program. This force consists of personnel who are specifically organized, trained, and equipped to protect the physical security interests of the facility.

Security Force Duties

Security force duties vary with the requirements of an installation or facility. However, all assigned duties should contribute to the physical security program. Within the scope of their authority, security forces achieve their purpose by a combination of actions consisting principally of the following:

1. Operate and enforce the system of personnel identification and movement control.
2. Observe and patrol designated perimeters, areas, structures, and activities of security interest.
3. Observe and patrol areas outside the perimeter.
4. Apprehend persons attempting or gaining unauthorized access to any portion of the installation or facility.
5. Check depositories, rooms, or buildings of security interest during other than normal working hours to determine that they are properly locked and are otherwise in order.
6. Perform escort duties for materiel or designated persons when required.
7. Enforce the established system of control over the removal of property and documents or materiel of security interest from the installation or facility as may be applicable. It may be necessary for security force personnel to establish the system and monitor its operation.

Figure 2. Apprehension of persons attempting or gaining unauthorized access to any portion of the installation is a basic function of security personnel.

8. Respond to protective alarm signals or other indications of suspicious activities.
9. Act as necessary in the event of situations affecting the security of the installation or facility (including fires, accidents, internal disorders, and attempts to commit espionage, sabotage, or other criminal acts).
10. Generally safeguard information, materiel, or equipment against sabotage, unauthorized access, loss, theft, or damage.
11. Operate and enforce regulatory traffic controls and procedures to maintain the smooth flow of traffic and to prevent or reduce the number of accidents.
12. Perform such other security duties outside the installation or facility as may be required; e.g., port and harbor security, loading/unloading operations aboard ships, security escort on lines of communication, and other duties required.
13. Report periodically, as a matter of prescribed routine under normal conditions, and as necessary in the event of unusual or emergency circumstances.

Selection

Regardless of the use of structural, mechanical, electronic, and other supplements, the human element in security operations makes the difference between success and failure. Administrators and supervisors have a definite responsibility to insure that security personnel who control access to restricted areas and classified activities are screened, selected, cleared, retained, or disqualified, based on criteria contained in government regulations, i.e., secret, top secret, etc.

Necessary Qualities of Security Force Personnel

Most of the qualities desired in security personnel are developed through training and become "instinctive" through experience. Every man assigned to security duties must recognize the part he plays in this development; he must have an awareness of his need to acquire these "instincts" and a desire for self-improvement. Many qualities are desirable for security personnel; those considered essential for effective performance of security duty are outlined below:

1. *Alertness.* This quality, more than any other, will determine the effectiveness of a person assigned to security force duties; it must be cultivated by all security force personnel. For example, even though hundreds of contacts are made with individuals who show proof of the right and need to enter a restricted area, one contact could be with a

person who should not enter. To detect this one exception, the security guard must be constantly alert. He must watch for deviations from the normal, such as a strange car near his post, a person approaching from an area which is not normally used, or nervousness in an approaching individual. Little things that seem to have no significance may add up to something important. Alertness is a combination of keen vigilance and diligent execution of the requirements of the patrol or post. Technological advances in communications equipment and protective alarm systems enhance the effectiveness of security forces, but there is no substitute for the alertness of security force personnel. Alertness makes the difference between effective security and a lack of security.

2. *Judgment.* Sound judgment is more than common sense; it is the ability to arrive at a wise decision. The process involves a mental comparison of an unfamiliar situation with a similar situation of known values and relationships. With discrimination during the process of elimination, the formulated decision will be sound. It follows that knowledge precedes judgment, and experience provides knowledge. Both are requisite. Security instructions cannot cover each situation; they can provide only fundamental guidelines because each situation is unique and requires individual consideration. Each man must develop the ability to observe, compare, and discriminate similarities and differences; and just as important, security personnel should be trained to call security headquarters for instructions when in doubt.

3. *Confidence.* Confidence is a state of mind free from doubt or misgivings. Confidence includes faith in oneself and in one's abilities, and nothing can bring about self-confidence like job knowledge. Each man must have confidence in himself, his weapons, and his leaders and other members of the security team. Confidence is thus best instilled with by thorough and proper training and competent supervision.

4. *Physical Fitness.* Security duty is difficult and demanding. The security of an installation or facility—and even the life of the person assigned to security duties—depend upon his physical fitness. Training in the techniques of unarmed defense and in physical conditioning is essential for developing this quality.

5. *Tactfulness.* The ability to deal with others without giving offense is essential: It is difficult to assume the authority and responsibilities of security duty without consciously or subconsciously displaying a sense of superiority and an overbearing manner. Security personnel must be able to give instructions clearly and concisely, firmly, and authoritatively, but without arrogance.

6. *Self-Control.* Security duty presents situations which require not only sound judgment and tact but also self-control. When an individual is offensive, the security man must be impersonal in his response or he will

likely lose control of his temper and of the situation. The security man, after he has given his instructions, should keep his conversation to a minimum. A person who is trying to "beat the system," will attempt to make the security man angry. A man on the defensive does not have the situation under control.

In selecting security personnel the man's general attitude towards life and the job is most important. Uncompromising interest and loyalty to the job are particularly applicable to security personnel. Supervisors must be alert for any change in this attitude which might adversely affect performance.

Women

Security positions that are not likely to require the use of physical force may be efficiently filled by women. These include such duties as checking passes at static posts, escorting visitors, and clerical and administrative duties in the security headquarters.

Organization and Employment of Security Forces

The organization of a security force depends on the circumstances and forces available. Forces may be organized by:

1. Fixed post deployment
2. Patrol deployment

The manpower requirements for a security force will vary according to the types of operations being performed. A method for computing requirements is shown in the following example.

1. Function: Physical security
2. Work activity: Fixed security post
3. Work unit: Fixed security post. It is operated on a continuing basis, 24 hours per day, 365 days per year, with 2 men on duty at the post at all times.
4. Performance standard: 52.8 man-hours per fixed post per day.
5. Productive hours per man per year: 2,753 man-hours, based on 12-hour shifts, 4,380 man-hours are available per man per year. Of this total, 1,627 man-hours are non-productive for duty, maintenance of equipment, briefing, travel to and from posts, and similar requirements.
6. Formula for determining authorization criteria:

Man-hours required per post per day × Operational days per post per year ÷ Productive man-hours per man per year = Number of direct workers required to man one post

7. Computation:

[52.8 × 365] ÷ 2,753 = 7 direct workers per post

8. Authorization criteria: 7 direct workers for each 2-man post.

9. Shifts: Security forces are normally organized into three or four shifts, usually on duty for eight-hour periods. Normally, one individual will be placed in charge of each shift of the force; clear and definite understanding should exist as to seniority and who is in charge of the shift. Changes of shifts should occur before peak periods of activity in the normal operation of the installation or facility. The minimum requirement of security personnel for each shift should be established by dividing the total number of man-hours needed by the hours in the shift. To this number must be added sufficient manpower to provide relief, which is usually based on one-half hour per man needed for each shift. If there is a post or patrol requiring less than 8 hours duty during a shift, this security may be provided by adding personnel to the shift and utilizing their services in some other post or patrol, or as relief during extra time.

Security Force Instructions

Instructions to the security force should be issued in writing. They should be reviewed at least monthly to be certain they are current.

A security force manual or handbook covering standing operation procedures, and setting forth policies, organization, authority, functions, and other required operating information, should be prepared and distributed to each member of the security force for required reading. Each man should be held responsible for full knowledge and understanding of its contents. Each installation chief of guard force should conduct periodic inspections and examinations to determine the individual's degree of understanding of and compliance with all security force instructions.

Security Force Headquarters and Shelters

The location of the security force headquarters will depend on the size and layout of the installation or activity. The objective is efficient control of the security force and adequate security of vital activities. On a small installation there is frequently only one full-time entrance, which may be supplemented by several part-time entrances. At such an installation the logical location of the headquarters would be at or near the main entrance. *or* On the other hand, at an installation of large acreage it might be much better located near the center of the main group of buildings.

The security force headquarters should be the control point for all matters pertaining to physical security of the installation and the terminal or monitoring point for protective alarm and communication systems. A list of key telephone numbers should also be available for use in emergency operations. It is frequently the office of record on security matters and usually houses the pass and badge office with its identification and visitor control files.

Personnel shelters should be basically designed to provide occasional temporary protection from severe weather. The design should normally include space for one person only; facilities such as heat, ventilation, storage space for essential accessories, lighting which will not expose the occupant, and good visibility in all directions.

Execution of Security Activities

Security personnel must clearly understand their relationship to employees. They have certain duties to carry out in respect to employees, but bad employee relationship can result if security personnel become officious and assume powers which are not rightfully theirs.

Security personnel must understand methods and techniques for detecting security hazards and assisting in identifying violators and intruders.

Written reports should be required for all security activities. These should be prepared by each man and turned in to the supervisor for necessary action.

Personnel assigned to fixed posts should have some prescribed method of securing relief when necessary. Where fixed posts do not permit the person to move at all, arrangements should be made so they may leave their posts at least every two hours.

A simple but effective plan of operation should be worked out for the security force to meet every foreseeable emergency. Practice alarms should be conducted frequently to test the effectiveness of this plan and the force's understanding of it. Such plans should be particularly designed to prevent a diversion at one point in the installation, drawing off the guards and distracting their attention from another section of the installation where unauthorized entry may be made.

Routes for security patrols should be varied at frequent intervals to preclude establishing a routine which may be observed by potential intruders and used to gain entrance.

Records of tours and reports to security headquarters should be carefully checked. Failure to record a visit at a designated station or to report to headquarters when required, or any other deviation from established reporting procedures should be investigated immediately. Security personnel should have no fire-fighting or other similar duties regularly assigned. Such emergencies offer an excellent diversion to cover the entrance of a pilferer. Consequently, during such times, security personnel should be exceptionally alert in the performance of their duties.

It must be strongly emphasized that security personnel will be used for security duties and should not be given other routine functions except as directed by the commander or his representative. They may and should, however, be given cross-training in other areas such as fire fighting so that they may be utilized when required and the circumstances permit.

Training

The extent and type of training required for security forces varies according to the importance, vulnerability, size, and other factors affecting a particular installation or facility. The objective of the training program is to insure that all personnel are able to perform routine duties competently and to meet emergencies quickly and efficiently.

Efficient and continuous training is the most effective means of obtaining and maintaining maximum proficiency of security force personnel. Regardless of how carefully a supervisor selects personnel for his force, it is unlikely that they will initially have all the qualifications and experience necessary to do the job well. In addition, new and revised job requirements frequently mean that personnel must be retrained for different jobs.

Supervisors must remember that all personnel do not have the same training needs. It is a waste of time to train an individual in that which he has already mastered, and it is frustrating to the man when he is subjected to instruction which he knows is not appropriate to his skill level. Past experience, training, acquired skills, and duty assignments should be evaluated for each man as an aid in planning an effective training program.

A good training program has benefits for both the installation and the security force. Some of these benefits are:

1. For supervisors—The task of supervising the security force is made easier: there is much less wasted time; there are fewer mistakes; the resulting economies of motion or action are of benefit to the installation; there is also less friction with other agencies. A good program also helps to instill confidence, which is most valuable to a security force.

2. For security personnel—Training increases the skills of personnel, thus increasing opportunities for promotion; and it provides for better understanding of their relationship to the management.

3. For the security organization—Good training helps to provide for more flexibility and better physical protection, fewer personnel may be required, and less time may be required for men to learn their duties and requirements. Training also helps to establish systematic and uniform work habits. An effective program will help to create better attitudes and morale.

Basic Training

1. Care and use of weapons—No man should be placed on security duty unless he has completed at least familiarization firing within the past 12 months with the weapon with which he is armed; weapons training must also include thorough indoctrination and understanding of the provisions concerning the use of force by security personnel.

2. Area of responsibility and authority of security personnel, particularly with regard to apprehension, search and seizure, and the use of force;

3. Location and use of first aid and fire control equipment and electrical switches;

4. Duties in event of emergencies, such as alerts, fire, explosion, civil disturbance, etc.;

5. Location of hazardous and vulnerable materiel.

In-Service Training

When a new individual is hired, he must be instructed in conditions peculiar to his post. Whenever possible, his first assignment should be with an experienced man. Additional in-service training and periodic retraining to review basic material and such other subjects as may be applicable to the specific installation is a continuous requirement for training supervisors.

The scheduling of classes for security forces is often difficult. It is commonly impossible to assemble an entire security force or even a complete shift at any one time to participate. As a result, the training supervisor must take care to provide an opportunity for each man to receive the training he needs.

Evaluation of Training

The use of tests or examinations to evaluate performance is a necessary step in the training program. These tests, which may be oral, written, or performance-type, should be given at least once a year to determine that high standards of proficiency are achieved and maintained by the entire force. A testing program will also aid in improving training by:

1. Discovering gaps in learning
2. Emphasizing main points
3. Evaluating instruction methods

Supervision

The physical security supervisor is responsible to management for the development of a security-minded organization. This development is greatly enhanced by a well-organized security education program.

The physical security supervisor's role is to advise on the formulation of policies for the physical security of an installation. His goal is the accomplishment of the assigned mission at the lowest possible cost consistent with policy. All physical security planners should remember that anyone can provide adequate security with unlimited funds; however, this is not a realistic approach. There must be a constant endeavor to effect justifiable economy wherever possible without jeopardizing the physical security program.

The Supervisor's Relationship with the Security Force

A security supervisor has the task of overseeing and directing the work and behavior of other members of the security force. The effective supervisor needs a complete understanding of the principles of leadership and how to apply them to obtain maximum performance from members of his force.

In addition to security interests, the security supervisor must be concerned with many other facets of his job: he is often responsible for the selection, induction, training, productivity, safety, morale, and advancement of the members of the force. He must manage these and all other employment aspects of his force.

To maintain an alert, presentable, efficient security force, supervision must be constant and constructive. Supervisors must be in evidence, and they must conduct themselves as models of neatness, fair play, efficiency, and loyalty—the morale and efficiency of a security force is a direct reflection of the quality of its supervision.

The ratio of supervisory to security personnel should be determined by the individual characteristics of each installation. In small, compact installations the ratio may be higher than at large installations. In general, there must be sufficient supervision to enable the inspection of each post and patrol twice per shift, plus sufficient back-up supervisory personnel to provide for sick and annual leave. It is also essential that supervisors be in contact with security headquarters to control emergencies that may arise. Specific duties of a supervisor include the inspection and briefing of the relief shift prior to its going on duty, and the inspection of posts, vehicles and equipment during visits to the posts and patrols.

Supervisors should strive for the creation and maintenance of a loyal force with high morale. Following are some of the means by which this may be accomplished:

1. Proper training and supervision;
2. Direction of the security force in an objective, business-like manner while exercising consideration for the personal welfare of the security force members;

3. Application of basic principles of human relations—the effective supervisor must know that there will be individual differences among members of his security force. He should be guided by the principle that subordinates are motivated in different ways; ambition can be stirred or pride hurt by his regard, or lack of it, for their welfare and feelings. A good supervisor must understand the needs and desires of each member of his force; he is their representative and they should be made to feel that he is the one with whom they can talk and discuss their problems, on a personal basis.

4. A good supervisor will develop versatility in his security force so that continuity of operations will be assured. He can do this by rotation of assignment, cross-training in varied duties, etc.

5. A good supervisor has the reputation of being honest, considerate, and willing to listen to both sides of a grievance. He must know his job and the principles involved and have the ability to teach these principles to his subordinates. All of these qualities will help greatly in building confidence among his personnel and securing their cooperation. Specific techniques for securing cooperation include the following:

—Each man should be made to feel his job is an important one.
—Each man should be given an opportunity to express his thoughts, likes, and interests to the supervisor.
—Supervision should be based on individual needs.
—Supervisors should recognize achievement. For example, a "security man of the month program" may be implemented, with appropriate reward for outstanding effort or achievement. achievement.
—Personnel may be recommended for advancement for outstanding effort.
—The supervisor should maintain an attitude of impartiality in dealing with his subordinates.

An effective supervisor develops good discipline by establishing rules which are just, complete, easy to administer, and understandable. If a supervisor needs to take corrective action involving his security force, it may only call for "setting a man straight," which is a recommended technique. Types of situations in which verbal corrective action should be considered are:

1. When the deficiency is due to lack of knowledge or training (this must be followed by appropriate training);
2. When the error is trivial;
3. When the action is a first offense;
4. When it is due to old habits (these must be corrected).

Under some circumstances the supervisor may need to take constructive disciplinary action. Occasions for this might be:

1. When verbal corrective action has failed;
2. In cases of flagrant or willful violation of installation or security rules;
3. When loss, damage or hazard is caused through negligence.

Disciplinary action should be handled calmly, in private surroundings, and the supervisor should know the facts. The supervisor should bear in mind the requirements for documented proof of events and actions that warrant disciplinary action. When the decision has been reached as to the propriety of probation or reprimand, further action should be pursued vigorously and without fear of reprisal or seemingly excessive administrative burden.

Supplements to Personal Supervision

Various means and devices may be used to supplement personnel supervision as a means of assuring that necessary areas are patrolled and other functions performed. These include:

1. Recorded tour systems, under which personnel record their patrols or presence at strategic points throughout an installation by use of portable watch clocks, central watch clock stations, or other similar devices. These effectively insure that such points are regularly covered, and they are useful at most installations, and facilities. This system provides an "after the fact" type of supervision.

2. Supervisory tour systems by which a signal is transmitted to a manned central headquarters at the time the tour station is visited. These have application at a limited number of installations to supplement personal supervision, or to supplant personal supervision at installations with small security forces.

3. All personnel on security duty should be required to report periodically to security headquarters by the usual means of communication. The frequency of such reports will vary depending on a number of factors, including the importance of the installation. Regularity should be avoided to preclude setting a pattern by which an intruder can gauge an appropriate time for entrance.

Security Force Problems

The security force must be effective at all times, regardless of the weather, the day, or the hour. This necessitates duty hours on weekends, holidays, and nights, and it can reduce enthusiasm for the job. The direct relation between quality of performance and morale demands consideration of these problems. The problem can be minimized by:

1. Maintaining high standards of discipline;
2. Promoting an aggressive security education program to insure that each man clearly understands the importance of his job. Each man must understand the consequence of any breach of protective barriers and that the human element in security operations makes the difference between success and failure.
3. Arranging shifts so that personnel will periodically have a 48-hour period from shift requirements.
4. Considering shift rotation as one solution to boredom. However, there are disadvantages which must be considered on the question of rotation of individuals from shift to shift. An advantage of permanent shift assignment is that each shift presents its own problems in security, and if the man is permanently assigned he learns these peculiarities and is able to cope with them more efficiently. Another advantage of regular assignment to the same shift is that the physical welfare of the man requires that he work regular hours and establish regular habits of eating and sleeping. The major disadvantage of being permanently assigned to one shift is that some shifts are considered very undesirable from the standpoint of hours of work.

The transfer of a man from one shift to another could be considered as reward, since the working hours of some shifts are more desirable than others. For better operation, the integrity of the shift should be maintained as a unit. In this way, each man will learn the abilities and limitations of the others, and will be able to function much more efficiently as a member of a coordinated team.

At installations or facilities where security force personnel are posted at exits/entrances or at other internal posts where they control the movement of traffic, they do not merely "stand guard." Such personnel check transportation movement documentation against actual loads on trucks; they check for hidden contraband, pilfered material, authorization for access onto or within the facility/installation, and safety violations; they conduct searches and seizures when authorized, and enforce regulations and assist visitors as appropriate. Men engaged in the performance of worthwhile duties do not become bored. When personnel are required to either stand or walk post merely as guards, especially in an oversea environment, they must be checked frequently for alertness. This requires aggressive and imaginative supervision, vulnerability tests, greater frequency in change of shifts, and even the rotation of personnel from one post to another within shifts as means of combatting boredom created by sedentary or otherwise unchallenging duties.

Equipment

All security force personnel should be required to wear the complete prescribed uniform. Deviations from the prescribed uniform requirements should not be made except for such additional items of wear as are necessary to protect the health, comfort, and safety of the individual.

The duty uniform should be worn during all tours of duty. Normally, it may be worn during off-duty hours only between the place of residence and place of duty. Each member of the security force should maintain high standards of personal and uniform appearance, and should wear a neat, clean, and well-pressed uniform.

Firearms

Security force personnel should be appropriately armed at all times while on duty. Normally, the weapon of issue will be a cal. 38. Weapons normally will be loaded with live ammunition, except where prohibited for safety reasons.

Weapons should be inspected at the beginning and end of each tour of duty, and at such other times as may be necessary to insure proper maintenance or to determine whether the weapon has been discharged. A written report should be prepared by the individual to whom the weapon was issued at the time it was discharged. Appropriate action should be taken in those instances when it is determined that the discharge of a weapon was not in the performance of assigned duties, or when it was the result of negligence.

Radio Equipment

The security force should be equipped with radio transmitters/receivers, both vehicle-mounted and portable, and telephones for quick transmission of reports and instructions between security headquarters, posts, and patrols. This equipment is essential for the efficient operation of the security force and the accomplishment of its assigned mission. Proper use and care by security personnel will enhance equipment usefulness and capability.

Miscellaneous Equipment

Security officers or supervisors should obtain such other equipment as may be necessary to implement their security program. Items in this category may include (but are not limited to): warning lights, sirens, and spotlights for vehicles; portable lights, flashlights;

first-aid kits; traffic-control devices; and items of wear for the health, comfort, or safety of security personnel.

Vulnerability Tests

Because of the routine, repetitious nature, and solitude of many security posts, personnel must make special efforts to overcome a tendency to relax in their performance of duties. To check on this weakness and keep personnel aware of their responsibilities, and as a means of pointing out other weaknesses in the security system, vulnerability tests may be used. These tests are normally designed by the physical security officer, and consist of attempts to breach security in one way or another, such as entering or attempting to enter a restricted area by means of deception. The types of deception which may be used are almost unlimited.

Test Objectives

A vulnerability test provides the management an estimate of the vulnerability of the installation or facility, tests the effectiveness of the security force and other personnel, alerts the personnel to the techniques that could be utilized by an intruder, and provides indications for corrective instruction. Specifically, the test should examine:

1. Improper enforcement of identification and control procedures by security personnel, such as failure to:
   —Determine authority for entry
   —Scrutinize identification media. The ways of using fake credentials to deceive security forces are numerous. The only way to detect such trickery is to know the details of each type of access credentials and to examine them thoroughly. Security tests and inspections have indicated that unauthorized persons have been granted access to restricted areas by altering or forging passes, by faking identification by telephone, and by playing upon the sympathy of security personnel with excuses.
   —Ascertain identity
   —Detain unauthorized persons
   —Conduct immediate preliminary search of suspects
   —Enforce security procedures
   —Report security violations

2. Susceptibility or gullibility of security personnel to plausible stories by intruders or members of the security force and other personnel of the installation. This inclination to believe, on slight evidence, an individual who may be attempting to gain unauthorized access to a restricted area is the product of two factors: monotony and a desire to save time. In the busy

activity of admitting individuals who have authorized access to a restricted area, it is easy for security personnel to be deceived by slight proof of authorization. The monotony of verifying hundreds of access credentials which are valid can dull the sensitivity to detect one which is invalid. Many attempts to deceive security personnel involve false credentials or falsely marked vehicles.

3. Unauthorized disclosure of information by members of the security force and other personnel of the installation.

Test Planning and Preparation

Detailed planning and preparation are required for effective testing of security. Planning should include:

1. Planning in secrecy in order to avoid alerting the personnel of the installation. Prior knowledge by the security forces or other personnel will produce invalid test results and thus defeat the purpose of the test.

2. Establishing a priority of targets that seem more vulnerable than others. Do not test the same target on a continuous basis. Attempt to test all eligible targets over a period of time. This will keep all personnel alert, rather than the personnel of only one area.

3. Selecting qualified personnel to conduct the vulnerability tests. Criteria for personnel should include:

—Appropriate security clearances for each member of the team at the same or higher classification level of the area or installation that might be entered. Such clearances preclude any compromise of security interest if a safe is found open or an area containing classified matter is entered.

—Members of the test team should be unknown to members of the security force or other personnel of the installation or facility.

—Team members should be capable of quick thinking in order to adapt to their cover stories.

—Team members should be able to bluff in a convincing manner.

—The cover story should originate with the physical security officer. A well-contrived cover story is necessary; it should sound convincing to provide an adequate test of the security force.

Test Instructions

The officer in charge of the test should select the method or techniques to be used. Instructions to team members should include the following:

1. Exploit any security weakness which becomes evident during the test.
2. Change tactics or take evasive action as necessary.
3. Strike targets of opportunity.

Personnel who are assigned to conduct vulnerability tests should be given only such information concerning the installation or facility that an outsider would normally have or could obtain through reasonable efforts.

Safety

Instructions to test team members should also include safety precautions. Test personnel should not:

1. Scale barriers of any kind, because the guards may fire;
2. Forcibly resist apprehension, because of the danger involved; by resisting apprehension, personnel will nullify benefits to be achieved;
3. Use any action which might affect the normal operations or the safety of equipment of the installation.

Techniques for Infiltrating Security Areas

Personnel conducting vulnerability tests should consider the following techniques for infiltration of security areas:

1. Entry through unguarded gates or open areas not under observation by security forces or other personnel;
2. The use of false or altered passes or badges through active gates that are manned by security personnel who give only a cursory glance at these credentials;
3. Entry through areas without presentation of identification media

   —One method is to bypass security forces by mingling with a work group entering the area.

   —Another method is to obtain permission to enter the area, claiming loss of identification media and using a plausible story.

   —A third method involves deception by false representation, whereby a member of the vulnerability test team poses as a high-ranking civilian dignitary, or as a repairman, installer of equipment, inspector, etc. who would have legitimate business in the area.

Review and Analysis of Vulnerability Tests

Upon completion of vulnerability tests, results should be reported, preferably in written form. The report should be carefully reviewed and analyzed by the physical security officer and others who may be responsible for physical security planning. The review and analysis should provide an evaluation of the physical security program and serve as a basis or guide for effecting necessary changes. It will also provide guidance for future tests.

Test results should be given appropriate security classification (should be the same as or higher than the security classification of the area). Dissemination of test results should be rigidly controlled and limited to those who have the required security clearance and a need to know.

Sentry Dogs (see p. 36-37)

The sentry dog, properly trained and utilized, can be a great asset to the physical security programs of some installations or facilities and should be considered in developing an effective crime prevention program. Use of the dog in conjunction with posting of conspicuous signs is a strong psychological deterrent to attempted intrusion.

The mission of the sentry dog is to detect intruders, alert his handler, and when necessary, pursue, attack, and hold any intruder who tries to escape. Normally, the dog has done his job by detecting the intruder and alerting the handler who is then responsible for taking appropriate action.

The sentry dog and the handler work as a team. Since the outstanding qualifications of the sentry dog for security duties are his keen senses of hearing and smell, he is used to most advantage during the hours of darkness or poor visibility, when human vision is restricted. Because of the added perception of the handler-dog patrol, patrol routes can often be lengthened without sacrificing coverage.

The sentry dog is used for exterior and interior security duty. This type of dog is trained to warn his handler by growling or barking, or by silent alert. He is almost always worked on a leash. The handler can depend on the dog to alert him to the approach or presence of strangers in or about the area being protected. When the dog alerts, the handler must be prepared to cope with the situation; that is, he must challenge, investigate, remain concealed, or apprehend. The dog, kept on leash and close to the handler, will also assist as a psychological factor in such circumstances. He will attack upon being released from the leash.

Sentry dog posts and patrols can be broken down into three types for reference and utilization. These are:

1. *Perimeter*. This type patrol is along a portion of, or the entire, fence line, either inside or outside, which may enclose security areas such as parking areas, storage areas, pipeline and pumping stations.

2. *Area*. This type post is located around a group of buildings which may be considered critical but do not justify perimeter posts. These posts are used for security in depth.

3. *Specific*. Buildings such as warehouses or offices which contain valuable or highly classified materials.

The sentry dog patrol is especially effective in areas of little activity such as isolated perimeters, remote storage areas, and open storage areas. The dog also tends to keep the man on post more alert, give him added self-assurance, and to relieve the ever-present monotony and loneliness of security duty.

In addition to a man-and-dog walking post, which is the most common and desired method, there are other methods of employing dogs. Some of these are:

1. As warehouse dogs. Dogs may be placed in warehouses at the close of the day, remain throughout the night, and then be taken out of the warehouse the next morning. This eliminates the necessity of having a guard stay with the dog all through the night, only requiring a roving patrol to check on the presence of the dog. The dog will alert the security force by barking at any attempt by intruders to enter his patrol area.

2. On cables which may be extended between two buildings or areas. The dog is hooked to this cable and is permitted to run.

3. In front of an entrance to a security area and will bark when anyone comes close.

4. In vehicles. While this method has not been widely used, it has possibilities for security force applications.

The proper utilization of the sentry dog depends upon the situation and the results desired, but normally the handler-dog patrol is the most effective method. Regardless of how the sentry dog is utilized, the mere knowledge by potential intruders that dogs are on duty in the area will have a great psychological effect and often be a deterrent in itself. A vicious dog is often more feared than an armed guard.

The sentry dog is a versatile animal, but he does have some limitations: The odor of petroleum products decreases the effectiveness of his sense of smell. Noise is a definite limitation, as it decreases his sense of hearing. Activity near a sentry dog post is also another limitation, as it tends to distract the dog.

Advantages

There are some definite advantages to incorporating the use of sentry dogs in a physical security plan to supplement the security force. Some of these advantages are:

1. Sentry dogs provide a very strong psychological deterrent to intruders.
2. They help when security forces have been reduced.
3. A dog's keen senses of smell and hearing enable him to detect danger and to alert his handler.
4. Safety—there is less chance of a fatality through the release of a dog than through firing a weapon at an intruder.

5. A dog can apprehend intruders during hours of darkness.

6. A dog is more effective than a man during inclement weather, an ideal time for illegal entry.

Disadvantages

There are problems inherent in the use of sentry dogs. Attrition and turnover of personnel trained as handlers reduce the efficiency of the dog program. Other problems include:

1. A break-in period is necessary to facilitate man and dog working as a team. This results in many nonproductive hours.

2. The type of dog best suited for security work is naturally dangerous. Care must be taken that innocent persons are not hurt.

3. Kennels and training areas must be isolated and kept off-limits to unauthorized persons. Signs should be posted warning of the presence of sentry dogs.

4. Care and maintenance of sentry dogs must be considered in manpower requirements. To maintain the physical fitness required of sentry dogs, the periodic services of a veterinarian are necessary.

5. Careful selection and training of handlers. The qualities of a handler dictate, to a great extent, the effectiveness of the sentry dog. Volunteers and personnel who like and understand dogs are not always available as handlers. There will be some morale problem among the handlers, as most of the work is at night and, in addition to security duty, they are normally required to care for and train their assigned dogs.

6. Public relations must be considered when planning for the use of dogs. Many persons feel strongly that using dogs for security or police purposes is brutal.

Although these problems must be considered, remember the value of the sentry dog. Any method of reinforcing available manpower, whether it be weapon, machine, or animal, should be carefully appraised. Man's capabilities will increase when his partner is a properly trained sentry dog. Used in conjunction with other physical safeguards, the sentry dog can be invaluable to the physical security program.

3

Physical Protection

Physical protection as used in this chapter generally refers to the physical safeguards used for the protection of a fixed installation or facility. Many of these measures may also be used in temporary situations, such as the establishment of perimeter barriers and utilization of movable protective lighting around a temporary facility or a facility under construction.

In his study and analysis of physical protection requirements, the physical security officer must use a systems approach to insure that all elements of the physical security plan are integrated and complement each other, since no single element can function properly by itself. Protective lighting is of little value except as a possible deterrent if the lighted areas are not under observation of the security force; alarms will serve no purpose if no one responds to them; and barriers will not be as effective if they are not patrolled and observed.

The physical security officer must also consider the cost of physical protection safeguards, and weigh those costs against other factors such as the criticality, vulnerability, location, and mission of the installation or facility.

Restricted Areas

A restricted area is any area access to which is subject to special restrictions or controls for reasons of security or safeguarding of property or materiel.

For a government security contract, a "restricted area" is *not* applicable to an area solely for the purpose of protection against common pilferage or misappropriation of property or materiel which is not classified or which is not essential to the national defense. For example, an area devoted to the storage or use of classified documents or materiel should be so designated to safeguard against espionage. An installation or a communications center should also be so designated, to safeguard against

38

sabotage. On the other hand, a cashier's cage or an ordinary mechanic's tool room should not be so designated, although security may impose controls on access thereto. This may be a simple matter of posting a sign, "Off Limits to Unauthorized Personnel," or it may require the erection of fences, railings, etc. The responsibility for designation is, of course, the company's.

The establishment of restricted areas improves security by providing defense in depth, and it increases efficiency by providing degrees of security compatible with operational requirements. These specially designated areas may also provide for economy of operation by reducing the need for stringent control measures for the installation or facility as a whole.

Types of Restricted Areas

The degree of security and controls required depend upon the nature, sensitivity, or importance of the security interest or other matter involved. Restricted areas may be established to provide:

1. Effective application of necessary security measures and exclusion of unauthorized personnel;
2. Intensified controls over those areas requiring special protection;
3. Conditions for compartmentalization of classified information or critical materiel, with a minimum impact on operations.

Different areas involve different degrees of security interest, depending upon their purpose and the nature of the work, information, and/or materiel concerned. In some cases, the entire area of an installation may have a uniform degree of importance, requiring only one level of restriction and control. In others, differences in degree of importance will require further segregation or compartmentalization of certain activities.

To meet these different levels of sensitivity and to provide an effective basis for applying the varying degrees of restriction of access, control of movement, and type of protection required, restricted areas or portions thereof may be further administratively designated as "exclusion," "limited" or "controlled" areas.

The primary criterion for the administrative designations of exclusion, limited, and controlled areas is the degree of restriction or controls required to prevent compromise of the security interest or other matter therein. Characteristics of these areas are:

1. *Exclusion area.* A restricted area containing

—A security interest or other matter which is of such nature that access to the area constitutes, for all practical purposes, access to such security interest or matter;

—A security interest or other matter of such vital importance that proximity resulting from access to the area is treated as equivalent to A the preceding. #1 above.

2. *Limited area.* A restricted area containing a security interest or other matter, in which uncontrolled movement will permit access to such security interest or matter, but within which access may be prevented by escort and other internal restrictions and controls. Individuals who have a legitimate reason for entering a limited area may do so if internal restrictions and controls are provided to prevent access to the security interest or other matter. These measures usually consist of escorts and other physical safeguards.

3. *Controlled area.* An area usually adjacent to or encompassing limited or exclusion areas. Access to the controlled area is restricted to those with a need for access. However, movement of authorized personnel within this area is not necessarily controlled, since mere access to the area does not provide access to the security interest or other matter within the exclusion or limited areas. The controlled area is provided for administrative control, safety, and/or as a buffer zone for depth in security for the exclusion or limited areas. The degree of control of movement within this area will, therefore, be as prescribed by the appropriate authority.

So, an installation may have varying degrees of security designation, or none at all. It may be designated in its entirety as a restricted area, with no further degree of restrictions or controls.

Other Considerations

There are other important considerations to keep in mind concerning restricted areas and their compartmentalization. Some are:

1. Immediate and anticipated needs. Immediate needs can be determined by survey and analysis of the installation or activity, its missions, and the security interests of other matters on hand which require protection. Anticipated needs can be determined from management's future plans.

2. The nature of the security interest or other matter to be protected. Small items may be protected by securing them in safes or locked containers, whereas large items may have to be placed within guarded enclosures.

3. Some security interests are more sensitive to compromise than others. Brief observation or a simple act by an untrained person may constitute a compromise in some cases. In others, detailed study and planned action by an expert may be required.

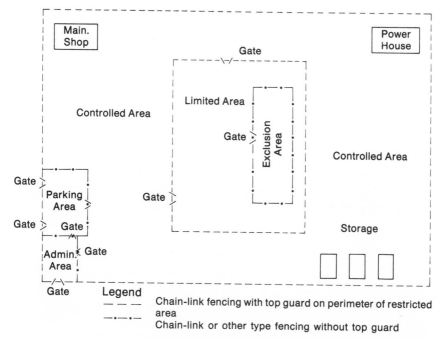

Figure 3. Schematic diagram of compartmentalization for physical security.

All security interests should be evaluated according to their relative importance. This may be indicated by a security classification.

Parking areas for privately-owned vehicles must be established outside restricted areas if at all possible because large amounts of articles can be readily concealed in vehicles and would then be harder to detect than if they were on a person. Also, entrances should be kept at a minimum necessary for safe and efficient operation and control.

The establishment of restricted areas within an installation improves overall security by providing defense in depth. The limited and exclusion areas serve as inner rings of defense; the controlled area serves as a buffer zone. As a general rule, an increase in security results in some slowdown in operations. The use of security areas makes it possible to have security compatible with operational requirements. Instead of establishing stringent control measures for the installation as a whole, varying degrees of security can be provided as required and as conditions warrant. In this way, interference with overall operations is reduced to a minimum and operational efficiency can be maintained at a relatively high level.

Where required, adequate physical safeguards such as fences, gates, and window bars must be installed to deny entry of unauthorized persons into restricted areas. Except where such action would tend to advertise an otherwise concealed area, warning signs or notices should be posted in conspicuous and appropriate places, such as ordinary entrances or approaches to these areas, and on perimeter fences or boundaries of the area.

Perimeter Barriers

A perimeter barrier is a medium which defines the physical limits of an installation or area and restricts or impedes access thereto. A perimeter barrier also:

1. Creates a physical and psychological deterrent to accidental entry to the area.
2. Deters unauthorized entry by covert means.
3. Delays intrusion into an area, making detection and apprehension by security force more likely.
4. Facilitates the effective utilization of security forces by economizing on the number of personnel required.
5. Directs the flow of persons and vehicles through designated entrances and facilitates identification and control procedures.

Types of Physical Barriers

Physical barriers may be of two general types: natural and structural. Natural barriers include mountains, cliffs, canyons, rivers, seas, marshes, deserts, or other terrain difficult to traverse. Structural barriers are manmade devices such as fences, walls, floors, roofs, grills, bars, road blocks, or other structures which deter penetration. To be fully effective, barriers must be under the surveillance of security forces and otherwise fully integrated into the physical security plan of the installation or facility. If a natural barrier forms any part of the perimeter, it in itself should not automatically be considered an adequate perimeter barrier, since it may be overcome by a determined intruder. Structural barriers should be provided for that portion of the perimeter, if required.

Use of Physical Barriers

Physical barriers should be used not only in the protection of the entire installation or facility but also in establishing restricted areas. The following guidance may be used for physical barriers in connection with the types of areas they serve:

The size of such areas, which in some cases may comprise extensive tracts of land, will depend upon the nature of the security considerations which may be the reasons for their establishment. These considerations will have a bearing on the essentialness and economic reasonability of the establishment of structural barriers on the outer perimeter. Defining the outer perimeter of a restricted area may be accomplished by:

1. Structural barriers at control points and other conveniently usable points of entrance and exit;

2. Natural and structural barriers between control points which are sufficiently obstructive and difficult to traverse to facilitate control and preclude accidental intrusion.

The size of restricted areas will depend on the degree of compartmentalization required and the complexity of the area. As a rule, the size should be kept to a minimum consistent with operational efficiency. Positive barriers should be established to provide for:

1. Controlling vehicular and pedestrian traffic flow;
2. Checking identification of personnel entering or departing;
3. Establishing a buffer zone for more highly classified areas;

Positive barriers are required for the entire perimeter of limited or exclusion areas. Specific types of barriers cannot be predesignated for all situations; however, they should incorporate the following elements:

1. Structural perimeter barriers, such as fences, walls, etc.;

2. Provisions at points of entrance and exit for identification checks by either badge exchange or badge examination;

3. Opaque barriers to preclude visual compromise by unauthorized personnel may be necessary in certain instances.

In situations wherein the nature of a secure area dictates a requirement for a limited or exclusion area on a temporary or infrequent basis, construction of physical perimeter barriers of the types described above is normally impractical or unjustified. In such cases, a temporary limited area or exclusion area may be established in which the lack of proper physical barriers is compensated for by additional security posts, patrols, and other compensation security measures during the period of restriction.

In evaluating the respective merits of wire fencing and other types of barriers, consideration should be given to the better visibility provided by a wire fence and the resultant probability of earlier detection of external approach.

Types of Fencing

The two types of fencing normally used are chain-link and barbed wire. Generally, chain-link fencing should be utilized for protection of permanent security areas; barbed wire for less permanent. Normally, outside perimeter fencing should be straight to permit unhampered observation; it should not be less than seven feet high; and when property lines and location of buildings permit, it should be no less than 50 feet from the object of protection.

Chain-link fence, including gates, should be no less than seven feet in height plus a top guard and with mesh openings not larger than two inches per side with a twisted and barbed selvage at top and bottom. It should be taut and securely fastened to rigid metal posts set in concrete. It should reach within two inches of hard ground or paving, and on soft ground should reach below the surface sufficiently to compensate for shifting soil or sand. Anti-erosion measures such as the use of surface priming may be necessary. Chain-link fencing is attractive, low in maintenance costs, less of a safety hazard because of its lack of barbs, and has openings small enough to prevent the passing of pilfered articles.

Standard barbed wire is twisted, double-strand, No. 12-gauge wire, intended to prevent human trespassing. It should be no less than seven feet in height plus a top guard, tightly stretched, and firmly affixed to posts not more than six feet apart. Distances between strands should not exceed six inches. Where the fencing is also intended to exclude small animals, the bottom strand should be at ground level to impede tunneling, and the distance between strands should be two inches at the bottom gradually increasing to six inches at the top. A top guard should be constructed on all vertical perimeter fences and on interior enclosures when added protection is desirable. A top guard is an overhang of barbed wire or tape along the top of a fence, facing outward and upward at an angle of 45 degrees. Three or four strands of barbed wire or tape, spaced six inches apart, are used, but the length of the supporting arms and the number of strands can be increased when required. The supporting arms are affixed to the top of the fence posts and are of sufficient height to increase the overall height of the fence at least one foot. Many fences employ a double overhang (overhang facing both outward and inward) which gives protection against the possibility of an individual leaving the installation by going over the fence. The overhang of top guard may be fixed or on springs. The spring-type overhang increases the difficulty of scaling the fence. Where a building of less than three stories forms a part of the perimeter, a top guard should be used along the outside coping to deny access to the roof.

Design of Physical Barriers

The following specifications are set forth as guidelines for those responsible for planning and designing physical barriers.

Fencing. Recommended fencing with specifications:

Figure 4. Physical barriers such as chain-link fences are an impediment to, but not an absolute protection against, intruders. Such barriers are only effective when they are frequently patrolled and inspected.

1. When property lines, location of installation, and adjacent structures permit, it should be located not less than 50 feet nor more than 150 feet from the location of interior buildings or object of protection.

2. Fencing should be arranged so there is at least 20 feet clearance between perimeter barriers and exterior structures, parking areas, or other natural or cultural features which would offer concealment or facilitate unauthorized access to the area protected. Where this is not possible due to property lines, the location of an installation, or adjacent structures, the perimeter barriers should be increased in height or otherwise designed to compensate for the proximity of such aids to concealment or vulnerability of the area to access.

Walls. Where walls, floors, roofs, doors or windows, or combinations thereof serve as barriers, they should be of such construction and so arranged as to provide uniform protection equivalent to that provided by chain-link fencing as specified. For example, when masonry walls provide the perimeter barrier, they should be of the minimum height specified for fencing and augmented by the barbed wire topping; when of less than the specified minimum height, they should be topped with chain-link fencing (or equivalent) to attain the minimum height requirements. As an alternative to the top guard or fencing, a masonry wall of eight feet or greater height may be topped with broken glass set on edge and cemented to the top surface. Where a fence adjoins a building wall, it should extend to within two inches of the building wall. Under some circumstances it may be desirable to increase the height of the fence gradually until it is double the original height at the point where it meets the building. Miscellaneous openings requiring adequate bar or grill protection include:

1. Openings less than 18 feet above uncontrolled ground, roofs, ledges, etc.;

2. Openings less than 14 feet directly or diagonally opposite uncontrolled windows in other walls, fire escapes, roofs, etc.;

3. All other openings having an area of 96 square inches or larger and a width of six inches or greater.

Bodies of Water

If a river or other body of water forms any part of the perimeter of an installation, it should not automatically be considered an adequate perimeter barrier. Additional security measures, such as a fence or frequent security police patrol and flood-lighting, may be necessary for those portions of the perimeter.

Perimeter Entrances

The number of gates and perimeter entrances in active use should be limited to the minimum required for the safe and efficient operation of the installation. Active perimeter entrances should be designated so that the security forces maintain full control without unnecessary delay in traffic. This is largely a matter of having sufficient entrances to accommodate the peak flow of both pedestrian and vehicular traffic, and adequate lighting for rapid and efficient inspection. When gates are not manned during nonduty hours, they should be securely locked, illuminated during hours of darkness, and periodically inspected by roving patrol; this applies as well to doors and windows which form a part of the perimeter.

Semiactive entrances, such as extra gates for use during peak traffic flow and railroad siding gates, should be locked at all times when not guarded. The keys to such entrances should be in the custody of the

Figure 5. Main perimeter entrances should be manned by security personnel on a full-time basis. Busy perimeter entrances should be designed so
that security forces can maintain full control without unnecessary delay in
traffic.

security officer or the chief of the security force and should be strictly
controlled.

Inactive entrances or those used only occasionally should be kept locked
and subject to the same key control and inspection as semiactive
entrances.

Sidewalk elevators and any other utility openings which provide access
to areas within the perimeter barrier should be locked, guarded, or
otherwise provided security equivalent to that of the perimeter barrier.

Security Control Stations

Security control stations normally should be provided at main perimeter entrances where such entrances are manned by security personnel on a full-time basis.

These control stations should be located as near as practicable to the perimeter entrance to permit personnel inside the station to maintain constant surveillance over the entrance and its approaches.

Security control stations which are manned 24 hours each day should be provided interior and exterior lighting, interior heating (where appropriate), and sufficient glassed area to afford adequate observation for the personnel inside. Where deemed appropriate, the stations should be designed for pedestrian movement control.

Perimeter Roads and Clear Zones

When the perimeter barrier encloses a large area, an interior all-weather perimeter road should be provided for security patrol vehicles. This road should be within the clear zone and as close to the perimeter barrier as possible.

Clear zones should be maintained on the sides of the perimeter barrier to provide an unobstructed view of the barrier and the ground adjacent thereto. Clear zones should be kept clear of weeds, rubbish, or other material capable of offering concealment or assistance to an intruder attempting to breach the barrier.

A clear zone of 20 feet or greater should exist between the perimeter barrier and exterior structures, parking areas, and natural or cultural features. When possible, a clear zone of 50 feet or greater should exist between the perimeter barrier and structures within the protected area, except when a building wall constitutes the perimeter barrier.

When it is impossible to have adequate clear zones because of property lines or natural or manmade features, an increase in the height of the perimeter barrier, increased security patrol coverage, more protective lighting, or an intrusion detection device along that portion of the perimeter barrier may be necessary.

Signs and Notices

Signs should be erected where necessary to assist in the control of authorized entry, to deter unauthorized entry, and to preclude accidental entry. Signs designed for this purpose should be plainly displayed and be legible at a reasonable distance from any approach to the perimeter. The size and color of such signs and the lettering thereon, as well as the interval of posting, must be appropriate to each situation.

Other Signs

Provision of entry. Signs setting forth the conditions of entry to an installation or area should be plainly posted at all principal entrances and should be legible under normal conditions at a distance not less than 50 feet from the point of entry. Such signs should inform the entrant of any provisions of search of the person, vehicle, packages, etc.; prohibitions against cameras, matches, lighters, and entry for reasons other than official business.

Restricted area. Signs or notices legibly setting forth the designation of restricted areas and provisions of entry thereto should be plainly posted at all entrances and at such other points along the perimeter line as are necessary.

Danger warning. It may be necessary, especially in situations where friendly children or young people approach perimeter barriers, to post signs warning them away from these barriers, particularly barbed wire or tape or glass-topped masonry walls.

Protective Lighting

Protective lighting provides a means of continuing during hours of darkness, a degree of protection approaching that which is maintained during daylight hours. This safeguard also has considerable value as a deterrent to thieves and vandals. It is an essential element of an integrated physical security program.

Requirements for protective lighting depend upon the situation and areas to be protected. Each situation requires careful study to provide the best visibility for such security duties as identification of badges and people at gates, inspection of vehicles, prevention of illegal entry, detection of intruders (both outside and inside buildings and other structures), and inspection of unusual or suspicious circumstances. Where such lighting provisions are impractical, additional security posts, patrols, sentry dog patrols, or other security measures may be necessary.

Specific Considerations for Planning

Generally, protective lighting is inexpensive to maintain and, when properly employed, may reduce the necessity for additional security forces and provide the present force more protection by reducing the chances of concealment and surprise by a determined intruder.

Normally, protective lighting requires less intensity than working light, except for identification and inspection at authorized portals and in emergencies. Each area of an installation or facility presents its particular problem based on the physical layout, terrain, atmospheric and climatic conditions, and the protective requirements. Data are available from the manufacturers of lighting equipment. Included in these data are:

1. Descriptions, characteristics, and specifications of the various incandescent arc, and gaseous discharge lamps;
2. Lighting patterns of the various luminaries;
3. Typical layouts showing the most efficient height and spacing of equipment;
4. Minimum protective lighting intensities required for various applications.

In planning a protective lighting system, the physical security officer must, in addition to the other factors discussed in this section, give specific consideration to the following:

1. Cleaning and replacing lamps and luminaries, particularly with respect to the costs and means (e.g. ladders, mechanical "buckets," etc.) required and available;
2. The advisability of including mercury and photoelectric controls;
3. The effects of local weather conditions on various types of lamps and luminaries;
4. Fluctuating or erratic voltages in the primary power source;
5. Grounding of fixtures and the use of a common ground on an entire line to provide a stable ground potential.

Fixtures

Fixture selection considerations are as follows:

1. Operating conditions
   —Subject to rough use—heavy-duty.
   —Exposed to severe atmospheric or corrosive conditions—heavy-duty.
   —Installation to be permanent—heavy-duty.
   —Light weight is a prime consideration—general purpose.

2. Elements
(*Note:* Iodine quartz is also referred to as "tungsten halogen.")
   —Greater number of burning hours per year—iodine quartz.
   —Lesser number of burning hours per year—incandescent.
   —For color clarity—incandescent, iodine quartz.
   —Low initial floodlight cost—iodine quartz.
   —Location subject to power failures—incandescent, iodine quartz.
   —Inaccessibility due to positioning—iodine quartz.
   —Lighting when rapid relight capability is not critical—gaseous lamps such as mercury vapor or fluorescent.

Note: Although gaseous filament lamps are capable of producing high light intensity, these lamps do not have an instantaneous relight capability. Depending on the type of lamp used, the relighting response may vary from 1 to 35 minutes. This response is also affected by weather conditions as well as the inherent delay features of the illumination material used in the lamp construction.

There are many commercially manufactured fixtures designed to provide adequate floodlighting. These fixtures can use either incandescent or iodine quartz lamps. Recent floodlighting design has produced fixtures that have an adjustable beam and use single-ended iodine quartz filaments. Another type of fixture is designed for use in glare-projection lighting. This type fixture uses incandescent bulbs but may be adapted for use with single-ended iodine quartz lamps.

The use of double-ended iodine quartz lamps is discouraged. Fixture mounting is critical for this type filament. The fixture must be mounted within four degrees of absolute level; any greater variation causes the light to fail since the gaseous substance of lamps will not provide an electrical bridge between the terminal poles of the filaments. This failure to complete the circuit causes the lamp to blacken and burn out rapidly.

Installation and Mounting

Fixtures may be mounted on poles singly or in clusters. By using conversion factors, a foot-candle chart may be used for various mounting heights. The foot-candle values vary inversely as the square of the mounting height, and the scale varies directly with the mounting height. The distance to the metering point varies directly with the mounting height.

Definitions

Candlepower: One candlepower is the amount of light emitted by one international candle or one standard candle. This measurement is made at the source of illumination. This is a standard characteristic of a lamp and may be determined from the manufacturer's description.

Foot-Candles: A light source of a given candlepower rating will produce the same foot-candle rating only on surfaces equidistant from the light source. Since the quality of light received at a surface varies inversely as the square of the distance between the source and the surface, the foot-candle value decreases as distance is increased.

Horizontal Illumination: Horizontal illumination is the illumination expressed in foot-candles on a horizontal surface. The surface is considered at ground level.

Vertical Illumination: Vertical illumination is the illumination expressed in foot-candles on a vertical surface.

Lumen: The quantity of light required to light an area of one square foot to one candlepower.

Brightness: The luminous intensity of any surface in a given direction. Brightness is one of the fundamental factors of seeing. Extremely high brightness in the visual field can cause glare and eye fatigue. When brightness values are low, seeing becomes difficult. To obtain good visibility, the brightness ratio of the visual task to its immediate surroundings should be no greater than three. A meter, known as the Luckiesh-Taylor brightness meter, can be used for direct measurement of brightness in foot-lamberts.

Foot-Lambert: A unit of brightness obtained when a diffusing surface of uniform brightness reflecting or emitting one lumen per square foot is viewed from a given direction.

Calculated Illumination: The estimated degree of illumination based on the results of photometric tests of individual units which are accurate within plus or minus two percent. These tests are based upon an average reflector which is absolutely clean, and tests are made under controlled laboratory conditions with new lamps selected and standardized for their rated lumen output. Calculated illumination should only be used for planning purposes. Field tests should be conducted to ascertain the effectiveness of light patterns. Individual fixture capabilities can be obtained from the manufacturer's specifications.

Photometer: All instruments used to check protective lighting systems should be capable of providing readable data and should have large-scale deflections for the values to be read. Of the equipment available, the Macbeth Illuminometer and the General Electric Low Range Sensitive Meter with the 0-2, 0-6, and 0-20 candle scales are considered acceptable.

The small meters used in photographic work should not be used; these are only accurate for measuring light which enters the cell perpendicular to its face. Protective lighting systems are designed to provide light from multiple sources. It is not practical to use a small meter by correcting for angular diviation. This cannot give comparative readings along a given line of lighting fixtures.

Principles of Protective Lighting

Protective lighting should enable guard force personnel to observe activities around or inside an installation without disclosing their presence. Adequate lighting for all approaches to an installation not only discourages attempted unauthorized entry but also reveals persons within the area. But lighting should not be used alone: it should be employed with other measures such as fixed security posts or patrols, fences, and alarms.

Good protective lighting is achieved by adequate, even light upon bordering areas, glaring lights in the eyes of the intruder, and relatively little light on the security patrol routes. In addition to seeing long distances, security forces must be able to see low contrasts, such as indistinct outlines of silhouettes, and must be able to spot an intruder who may be exposed to view for only a few seconds. All of these abilities are improved by higher levels of brightness.

In planning to provide protective lighting, high brightness contrast between intruder and background should be the first consideration. With predominantly dark, dirty, surfaces or camouflage-type painted surfaces, more light is needed to produce the same brightness around installations and buildings than where clean concrete, light brick and grass predominate. When the same amount of light falls on an object and its background, the observer must depend on contrasts in the amount of light reflected. The ability of the observer to distinguish poor contrasts is significantly improved by increasing the level of illumination. When the intruder is darker than his background, the observer sees primarily the outline or silhouette. Intruders who depend on dark clothing and even darkened face and hands may be fooled if light finishes are used on the lower parts of buildings and structures. Stripes on walls have also been used effectively, as they provide recognizable breaks in outlines or silhouettes. Good observation conditions can also be created by providing broad lighted areas around and within the installation against which intruders can be seen.

Two basic systems, or a combination of both, may be used to provide practical and effective protective lighting. The first method is to light the boundaries and approaches; the second, to light the area and structure within the general boundaries of the property.

To be effective, protective lighting should

1. Discourage or deter attempts at entry by intruders. Proper illumination may lead a potential intruder to believe detection inevitable.

2. Make detection likely if entry is attempted.

Illumination Arrangement

Insofar as possible, the cone of illumination from lighting units should be directed downward and away from the structure, or area protected, and away from the security personnel assigned to such protection. The lighting should be so arranged to create a minimum of glare in the eyes of guards.

Lighting units for restricted area perimeter fence lighting should be located a sufficient distance from the protected area and above the fence so that the light pattern on the ground will include an area on both the inside and outside of the fence. Generally, the light band should illuminate the restricted area and extend as deeply as possible into the approach area. Factors such as adjacent waterways, highways, railroads, and residences, may limit the depth of the light band.

When determining the location of illuminating fixtures along the fence, care must be taken to insure that the poles which mount the fixtures are located far enough behind the inner fence, to insure that they do not become a means of assisting an intruder in scaling or otherwise breaching the fence.

Backgrounds

Indirect interior lighting makes use of the ceilings and upper sidewalls of a room for redirecting and diffusing light given by lamps. This is in part a matter of the light-reflecting properties of various colored surfaces. The same is true of exterior lighting. Dark areas are the ally of an intruder. To permit a guard to see an intruder crossing a dark strip outside a perimeter fence, or passing in front of a grey-black wall of a building, much more light is required than if both backgrounds were light in color. An eight-foot strip of white sand outside the perimeter fence, or a light-colored wall, will permit better visibility with less expenditure of light. In areas where there is little traffic by authorized personnel a background of alternating light and dark strips on the ground or on the building wall will aid in the detection of movement, but supplementary light must be available for more detailed examinations.

Types of Protective Lighting

The type of lighting system to be used will depend upon the overall security requirements of the installation. Lighting units of four general types are used for protective lighting systems.

1. *Continuous Lighting (Stationary Luminary)*. This is the most common protective lighting system. It consists of a series of fixed luminaries arranged to flood a given area continuously with overlapping cones of light during the hours of darkness. Two primary methods of employing continuous lighting are glare-projection and controlled lighting.

—Glare-projection lighting. This method is useful where the glare of lights directed across surrounding territory will not be annoying nor interfere with adjacent operations. It is a strong deterrent to the potential intruder because it makes it difficult for him to see the inside of the area. It also protects the guard by keeping him in comparative darkness while enabling him to observe intruders at considerable distance beyond the perimeter. Floodlights (Figure 6)

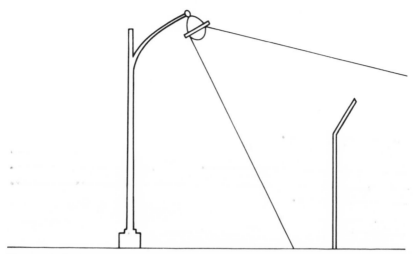

Figure 6. Perimeter protection by glare-projection lighting. This type of lighting is a strong deterrent to intruders because it makes seeing inside the perimeter difficult.

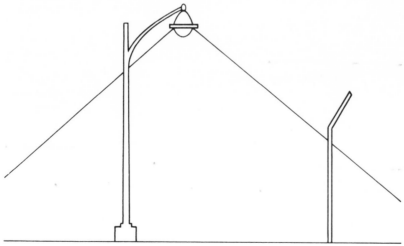

Figure 7. Perimeter protection by controlled illumination lighting.

which provide a band of light whose horizontal angular dispersal is great, and which direct the glare at a possible intruder while restricting the downward beam, are the preferred lighting in this application.

—Controlled lighting. Where it may be necessary to limit the width of the lighted strip outside the perimeter because of adjoining property or nearby highways, railroads, navigable waters, or airports, controlled illumination will be required. In controlled lighting, the width of the lighted strip can be controlled and adjusted to fit the particular need, such as the illumination of a wide strip inside a fence and a narrow strip outside, or the floodlighting of a wall or roof. This method of lighting often illuminates or silhouettes security personnel as they patrol their routes (see Figure 7).

2. *Standby Lighting (Stationary Luminary)*. The layout of this system is similar to continuous lighting as above. However, the luminaries are not continuously lighted but are either automatically or manually turned on only at such times as suspicious activity is detected or suspected by the security force or alarm systems.

3. *Movable Lighting (Stationary or Portable)*. This type of system consists of manually-operated movable searchlights which may be lighted during hours of darkness or lighted only as needed.

4. *Emergency Lighting*. This type of system may duplicate any or all of the above systems. Its use is limited to times of power failure or other emergencies which render the normal system inoperative. It depends on an alternative power source, such as installed or portable generators or batteries.

Types of Light Sources

The object of lighting is to obtain the level of illumination required for the specific job to be accomplished. For instance, the glare-projection method of lighting is for perimeter protection under particular circumstances, whereas diffused light gives freedom from glare and is generally applicable when glare-projection is objectionable. The principal types of lamps used in protective lighting are:

1. *Incandescent Lamps*. These are common glass light bulbs in which the light is produced by the resistance of a filament to an electric current. Special-purpose bulbs are manufactured with interior coatings to reflect the light, with a built-in lens to direct or diffuse the light; or, the naked bulb can be enclosed in a shade or fixture to accomplish similar results.

2. *Gaseous Discharge Lamps*.

—Mercury vapor lamps emit a blue-green light caused by an electric current passing through a tube of conducting and luminous gas. They are more efficient than incandescent lamps of comparable wattage and are in widespread use for interior and exterior lighting, especially where people are working.

—Sodium vapor lamps are constructed on the same general principle as mercury vapor lamps but emit a golden yellow glow. They are more efficient than the other two types, and are used where the color is acceptable, such as on streets, roads, and bridges.

—Metal halide lamps emit a harsh yellow-colored light. They employ sodium, thallium, indium, and mercury.

—Fluorescent Lamps. These are large, elongated bulbs (up to nine inches long) which provide a high light output and have a recoverage light life of 7,500 hours. They have a higher initial cost but a lower operating cost than incandescent lamps.

Lighting Requirements

Appropriate protective lighting should be employed at all pedestrian and vehicular entrances where security personnel are stationed to check identification of personnel and vehicle loads.

Protective lighting should not be used as a psychological deterrent only: it should be used on a perimeter fence line only where the fence line is under continuous or periodic observation. Protective lighting may be unnecessary where the perimeter fence line is protected by a central station alarm system.

Protective lighting may be desirable for those sensitive areas or structures located within the perimeter which are under specific observation. Such areas or structures include pier and dock areas, vital buildings, storage areas, and vulnerable control points in communication, power, and water distribution systems. In interior areas where night operations are conducted adequate lighting of the area facilitates the detection of unauthorized persons approaching or attempting malicious acts within the area.

Under certain circumstances, restricted areas may be located and operated so as to attract a minimum of attention. Such areas may be provided with a protective lighting system, which is normally not lighted but will provide illumination in the event of local emergencies or suspicious activity in or near the area. These areas should also have an alarm system to overcome the security limitations of guarding in darkness.

Parking lots should be well lighted. In addition to the security hazard of providing hiding places, parking lots are vulnerable to pilferers, and attacks on employees are often made there. Good lighting helps reduce these hazards.

Lighting Specifications

A lighting specification table with guidelines for classification of areas, type lighting, and width of lighted strip inside and outside the fence is included at the end of this section.

The perimeter is considered to be the installation property line unless a fence is established inside the property line, in which case the fence will be considered the perimeter. Fenced perimeters are classified as follows:

1. *Isolated fenced perimeters* are fence lines around areas where the fence is 100 feet or more from buildings or operating areas, and where the approach area is clear of obstruction for 100 or more feet outside the fence and is not used by other personnel. In general, both glare-projection and controlled illumination are acceptable for these perimeters. In either case patrol roads and paths should be kept unlighted.

2. *Semi-isolated fenced perimeters* are fence lines where approach areas are clear of obstruction for 60 to 100 feet outside the fence and the general public or installation personnel seldom have reason to be in this area. Patrol roads and paths should be kept in relative darkness.

3. *Nonisolated fence perimeters* are fence lines immediately adjacent to operating areas within the installation, other installations, or to other thoroughfares, where outsiders or installation personnel may move about freely in the approach area. The width of the lighted strip in this case depends upon the relative clear zone inside and outside the fence. It may not be practicable to keep the patrol area dark.

Building face perimeters consist of faces of buildings which are on or within 20 feet of the property line or area line to be protected, and where the public may approach the buildings. Guards may be stationed inside or outside of the buildings. Doorways or other insets in the building's face should receive special attention for lighting to eliminate shadows.

Active entrances, pedestrian and conveyance, should be provided with two or more lighting units and with adequate illumination for recognition of persons and examination of credentials. All conveyance entrances should have two lighting units so located as to facilitate complete inspection of passenger cars, trucks, and freight cars as well as their contents and passengers. Semiactive and inactive entrances should have the same degree of continous lighting as the remainder of the perimeter, with standby lighting of sufficient illumination to be used when the entrance becomes active. Gate houses at entrances should have a low level of interior illumination to enable guards to see better and increase their night vision adaptability.

The illumination of open yards and of outdoor storage spaces should be as follows:

1. The illumination of open yards adjacent to a perimeter (between guards and fences) should be in accordance with the illumination requirements of the perimeter. Where lighting is deemed necessary in other open yards, the illumination should not be less than 0.2 foot-candle at any point.

2. Lighting units should be so placed in outdoor storage spaces as to provide an adequate distribution of light in aisles, passageways, and recesses, to eliminate shadowed areas where unauthorized persons may conceal themselves.

Piers and docks located on an installation should be safeguarded by illuminating both the water approaches and the pier area. Decks of open piers should be illuminated to at least 1.0 foot-candle and the water approaches (extending to a distance of 100 feet from the pier) to at least 0.5 foot-candle. The area beneath the pier flooring should be lighted with low-wattage floodlights arranged to the best advantage with respect to piling. Movable lighting that can be directed as required by the guards is recommended as a part of the protective lighting system for piers and docks. The lighting must not in any way violate marine rules, and regulations, nor be glaring to pilots. The United States Coast Guard should be consulted for approval of proposed protective lighting adjacent to navigable waters.

Critical structures and areas should be the first consideration in designing protective fencing and lighting. Power, heat, water, communications, explosive materials, critical materials, delicate machinery, areas where highly classified material is stored or produced, and valuable finished products all need special attention. Critical structures or areas which are classified as vulnerable from a distance should be kept dark (standby lighting available), and those which can be damaged close at hand should be well lighted. The surroundings should be well lighted to force an intruder to cross a light area, and the walls (if a building) should be lighted to a height of eight feet to facilitate silhouette vision.

Wiring Systems

Both multiple and series circuits may be utilized to advantage in protective lighting systems, depending upon the type of luminary used and other design features of the system. The circuit should be so arranged that failure of any one lamp will not leave a large portion of the perimeter line or a major segment of a critical or vulnerable position in darkness. Connections should be such that normal interruptions caused by overloads, industrial accidents, and building or brush fires, will not interrupt the protective system. In addition, feeder lines should be located underground or sufficiently inside the perimeter in the case of overhead wiring so as to minimize the possibility of vandalism from outside the perimeter. The design should provide for simplicity and economy in system maintenance and should require a minimum of shutdowns for routine repairs, cleaning, and lamp replacement. It may be necessary in some instances to install a duplicate wiring system, particularly where a series circuit is employed to preclude against loss of illumination due to a break in the primary line.

Maintenance

Periodic inspections should be made of all electrical circuits to replace or repair worn parts, tighten connections, and check insulation. Luminaries should be kept clean and properly aimed. Lamps of the protective system should be scheduled for group replacement at about 80 percent of their rated life. Lamps so replaced can be used in less sensitive locations. The actuating relays on emergency lines, which remain open when the system is operating from the primary source, need to be cleaned frequently since dust and lint will collect on their contact points and prevent their operation when closed. The intensity of illumination for protective lighting for fence or other antipersonnel barriers should meet the following minimum requirements:

Location	Foot-candles on horizontal plane at ground level
Perimeter of outer area	0.15
Perimeter of restricted area	0.4
Vehicular entrances	1.0
Pedestrian entrances	2.0
Sensitive inner area	0.15
Sensitive inner structure	1.0

Lighting Specification Table

Type of area	Type of lighting	Width of lighted strip (ft)	
		Inside fence	Outside fence
Isolated perimeter	Glare	25	200
Isolated perimeter	Controlled	10	70
Semi-isolated perimeter	Controlled	10	70
Non-isolated perimeter	Controlled	20-30	30-40
Building face perimeter	Controlled	50 (total width from building face)	
Vehicle entrance	Controlled	50	50
Pedestrian entrance	Controlled	25	25
Railroad entrances	Controlled	50	50
Vital structures	Controlled	50 (total width from structure)	

Protective Alarms and Communications Systems

Protective alarm systems are used to:

1. Economize—permit more economical and efficient use of manpower by substitution of mobile responding guard units for larger numbers of patrols and fixed guard posts.

2. Substitute—substitute for other physical security measures which cannot be used because of safety regulations, operational requirements, appearance, layout, cost, or other reasons.

3. Supplement—provide additional controls at critical points or areas.

Such intrusion-detection alarm systems may be installed outdoors or within structures, or both. These alarm systems are designed to alert security personnel to intrusion or attempted intrusion into an area or to tampering by an individual attempting to circumvent the intrusion-detection system. The use of these mechanical and electronic warning systems has proven beneficial in many situations; however, individuals responsible for physical security planning must be aware of the advantages and limitations of these devices so that they can be incorporated effectively into the security plan.

There are a variety of devices available which are designed to detect approach or intrusion. Others are continually being developed. Certain types of systems are suitable only for exterior protection, while others are suitable only for interior uses. All have weak points by which their functioning can be hampered or possibly stopped completely. It is important for planners to remember that any warning system is valueless unless it is supported by prompt security force action in the event of actuation of the alarm.

Determination of Necessity and Feasibility

To determine the necessity and feasibility of installing an alarm system, the following factors must be considered:

1. Vulnerability of the installation or facility;
2. Accessibility to intruders;
3. Location of installation or facility (geographical) and locations of areas to be protected inside the installation;
4. Construction of building;
5. Hours of operation;
6. Availability of other forms of protection;
7. Initial and recurring cost of alarm system as compared to cost in money or security of possible loss of materials or information;
8. Design and salvage value of the alarm system;

9. Response time by the security force;
10. Savings in manpower and money over a period of time.

Selection

Each type of intrusion-detection system is intended to meet a specific type of problem. Factors to be considered in selecting the appropriate system include (but are not limited to) the following:

1. Response time capability of security personnel;
2. Intruder time requirement;
3. Area environment, to include building construction, sound levels inside and outside, climate, etc.;
4. Radio and electric interference;
5. Operational hours of the installation or facility.

A consideration of these factors readily indicates the advisability of obtaining engineering studies to assist in making a wise selection. Often more than one system is necessary to give adequate protection for an area or structure.

Definitions

The following definitions are provided for common understanding of intrusion-detection devices.

Alarm Systems: Combinations of detection and alarm-signaling devices, means of signal transmission, and means of annunciating the alarm, with supporting functions, integrated to perform as required.

Annunciator (Monitor): A visual or audible signaling device which indicates conditions of associated circuits. Usually this is accomplished by the activation of a signal lamp and by audible sound.

Antenna: A conductor or system of conductors for radiating or receiving electromagnetic waves.

Intrusion-Detection Devices: Devices which initiate alarm signals as a result of sensing the stimulus of coordination to which they are designed to react.

Capacitance: The property of two or more bodies which enables them to store electrical energy in an electrostatic field between them.

Control Unit (also referred to as *Monitor Panel or Console*): A facility, consisting of switches, potentiometers, and audible and visible alarms, together with the system "on-off" switch, and possibly an annunciator system where more than one circuit is monitored; usually installed at a point manned full-time.

Fail-Safe: A term applied to a device or system so designed that in the event of a failure of some component the device will, by a signal or otherwise, indicate its incapacity.

Conductor: Material which transmits electric current; wire and cable are conductors.

Receiver: An electromechanical device for detecting and converting electromagnetic energy from a transmitter into sound waves.

Supervised Line: Connecting cable or wire which, if cut, broken, shorted, or grounded, will so indicate at a monitoring location.

Sonic: Having a frequency within the audibility range of the human ear.

Ultrasonic: The frequency range of sound that is above the capabilities of normal human hearing. In intrusion-detection systems application is usually considered as 19,200 cycles per second (also referred to as "supersonic").

Microwave: Having a frequency range of 10.5 million cycles per second.

Transmitter: The apparatus for converting sound waves into electrical waves.

Transducer: A device that transfers or changes one type of energy into another. An example is a loud-speaker which changes electrical into acoustical (mechanical) energy.

Underload: Less than a normal amount of current flowing through an electrical device.

Alarm Report System

Alarm and communications systems are closely allied in any comprehensive protection system. Telephone and radio communications are so commonly used that their adaptation to a protective system poses few new problems. An alarm system is simply a manual or automatic means of communicating a warning of potential or present danger. Types of alarm systems include:

1. *Local Alarm Systems.* A local alarm system is one in which the protective circuits or devices actuate a visual or audible signal located in the immediate vicinity of the object of protection. Response is by the local security or other personnel within sight or hearing. The light or sound device should be displayed on the exterior of the building, should be fully protected against weather or willful tampering, should be connected to the control element by a tamperproof cable, and should be visible or audible for a distance of at least 400 feet. This system can also be used in conjunction with a proprietary system, as described below.

2. *Auxiliary System.* An auxiliary system is one in which the installation-owned system is a direct extension of the police and/or fire alarm systems. This is the least effective system, and because of dual

responsibility for maintenance, it is not favorably considered by many protective organizations.

3. *Central Station System.* A commercial agency may contract to provide electric protective services to its clients by use of a central station system. The agency designs, installs, maintains, and operates underwriter-approved systems to safeguard against fire, theft, and intrusion, and it monitors industrial processes. Alarms are transmitted to a central station outside the installation from which appropriate action is taken, such as notifying local police or fire departments. Most agencies also have their own private police who are dispatched to the scene upon receipt of an alarm. Local audible signals can also be provided to alert occupants of the installation.

4. *Fail-Safe Features.* These give an alarm signal at the annunciator panelboard when abnormal operating conditions keep the alarm system from functioning properly.

5. *Features which make the system less vulnerable to persons trained to circumvent intrusion-detection systems.* Such features should include capability of concealment of the equipment and difficulty of neutralization of the system.

There are two basic means of providing security for alarm systems. First, security is provided by built-in technological security measures; i.e. as more technology (sophistication) is built into a system, more technology is required to breach or defeat the system. However, as more technology is built into a system, the cost of the system and the cost of maintenance usually increase accordingly. Second, security is provided by the use of physical security measures; i.e., the height of reporting lines on poles or the depth they are buried in the ground, control of access to the system equipment, etc. Physical security measures should be applied in inverse proportion to the built-in technological and physical security measures, at the lowest costs.

Principles of Operation

Depending on effectiveness, reliability, cost and maintenance required, intrusion-detection devices have varying degrees of acceptability. No one system is suitable or adaptable to every location and environment. The situations and conditions at the particular site to be protected determine which devices or systems are efficient and practical.

Some of the basic principles upon which these devices operate are:

1. Breaking of an electric circuit
2. Interruption of a light beam
3. Detection of sound

4. Detection of vibration
5. Detection of motion
6. Detection of capacitance change due to penetration in an electronic field

Breaking of an Electric Circuit

Possible points of entry into buildings or enclosures can be wired by using electrically charged strips of tinfoil or wire. An action which breaks the foil or wire interrupts the circuit and actuates an alarm. Foil stripping is frequently used on windowpanes. Doors and windows may be equipped with magnetic or spring-activated contacts which sound an alarm when the door or window is opened. Protective wiring running through concealed wooden dowels may be used on walls and ceilings.

Advantages
1. Consistently provides the most trouble-free service;
2. Causes few, if any, nuisance alarms;
3. Adequate in low-risk applications.

Disadvantages:
1. Costly to install for many entry points;
2. Lowest grade of recognized protection;
3. Easily compromised; unprotected soft walls or ceilings may be penetrated without disturbing the alarm system; it may also be defeated by bridging the circuits;
4. Usually of lesser quality because of highly competitive price markets and lack of standards required;
5. Has little salvage value—not recoverable;
6. Will not detect "stay-behinds."

Interruption of a Light Beam

The photoelectric (electric eye) type of intrusion-detection derives its name from the use of a light-sensitive cell and a projected light source. A light beam is transmitted at a frequency of several hundred vibrations per second. An infrared filter over the light source makes the beam invisible to intruders. A light beam with a differenct frequency (such as a flashlight) cannot be substituted for this beam. The beam is projected from a hidden source and may be criss-crossed in a protected area by means of hidden mirrors (Fig. 3) until it contacts a light-sensitive cell. This device is connected by wires to a control station. When an intruder crosses the beam, he breaks contact with the photoelectric cell, which activates an alarm. A projected beam of invisible light is effective for approximately

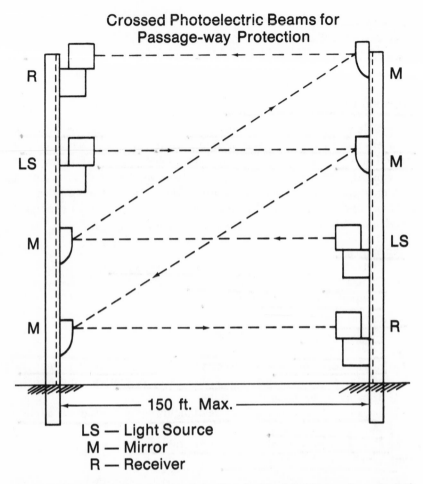

Crossed Photoelectric Beams for Passage-way Protection

— 150 ft. Max. —

LS — Light Source
M — Mirror
R — Receiver

Figure 8. Photoelectric intrusion-detection device. A light beam is projected from a hidden source and can be criss-crossed by means of hidden mirrors until it contacts a light-sensitive cell. An intruder crossing the beam breaks light contact with the cell, which activates an alarm.

500 feet indoors and 1,000 feet outdoors. The effectiveness of the beam is decreased approximately 30 percent for each mirror used.

Advantages:
1. When properly employed, affords effective, reliable notice of intrusion;
2. Useful in open portals or driveways where obstructions cannot be used;
3. Detects the "stay-behind";
4. Has a high salvage value; almost all equipment is recoverable;

5. May be used to actuate other security devices, such as cameras;
6. May detect fires through smoke interruption of the beam.

Disadvantages:
1. Employment is limited to those locations where it is not possible to bypass the beam by crawling under or climbing over it;
2. Requires some type of permanent installation;
3. Fog, smoke, dust, and rain in sufficient density will cause interruption of the light beam;
4. Requires frequent inspections of light-producing components to detect deterioration;
5. Requires keeping the ground beneath the light beam free of tall grass and weeds and drifting snow and sand;
6. Requires auxiliary power;
7. Subject to equipment failure.

Detection of Sound or Vibration

These types of protective devices can be effectively utilized to safeguard enclosed areas, vaults, safes, deposit storage bins, warehouses, and similar enclosures. Supersensitive microphones are installed in the area on the walls, ceilings, and floors. These detect sound or vibrations of sound caused by attempts to force entry into the protected area.

Advantages:
1. Economical and easily installed;
2. After an alarm is received, the amplifier may be adjusted to monitor sounds emanating from the protected area.

Disadvantages:
1. Can be used only in vault-type installations or other enclosed areas where a minimum of extraneous sound exists;
2. Not satisfactory where high noise levels are encountered, especially in proximity to heavy construction, aircraft, automotive and other traffic;
3. Cannot be used effectively outdoors.

Detection of Motion

The ultrasonic or microwave type of detection device is useful in building-type enclosures. It utilizes ultrasonic waves or microwaves. The sound waves saturate the entire enclosure from floor to ceiling. The transmitter is a small metal case mounted on a wall or ceiling. Its receiver is mounted similarly and it "listens" continuously to the sound being broadcast by the transmitter. It "hears" not only what is coming directly from the transmitter but also the "echoes" that bounce from walls, furniture, and other objects in the area. When motion disturbs the sound

Figure 9. A typical sound-detection device. Supersensitive microphones detect sound or vibrations of sound caused by attempts to force entry into the protected area. (Courtesy NOVAR Electronics Corporation, Barberton, Ohio.)

pattern, the resulting change in ultrasonic or microwave frequency activates a triggering device that signals the control station. Enclosures having a floor area of as much as 4,000 square feet can be covered by a single transmitter and reciever unit. Additional transmitter and reciever units may be added.

Advantages:
1. Requires minimum installation time;
2. Low routine maintenance cost;
3. If security interest terminates, complete recovery of equipment is possible.

Disadvantages:
1. Sensitivity controls must be carefully adjusted and frequently checked;
2. Nuisance alarms may lead security personnel to reduce the system's sensitivity;
3. At low sensitivity it is sometimes possible to enter a protected area without activating the alarm by staying beneath the level of tables or desks and by moving so slowly that the ultrasonic vibrations are not shifted;
4. May not be adaptable for use in areas where quantities of absorbent materials are stored since they absorb sound waves.

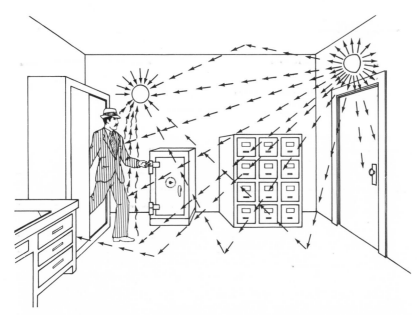

Figure 10. Ultrasonic or microwave motion-detection device. Transmitter mounted on ceiling saturates protected area with sound waves. When motion disturbs the sound pattern, an alarm device is activated.

Capacitance Change Due to Penetration of an Electronic Field

The electromagnetic or capacitance-type device can be installed on a fence, a safe, or in a building. It emits radio waves to establish an electronic field around the object to be protected. This field is "tuned" by a balance between the electric capacitance and the electric inductance. The body capacitance of any intruder who enters the field of radio waves unbalances the electromagnetic energy of the field. This unbalancing activates the alarm. Electromagnetic systems appear to offer the greatest potential for the development of truly satisfactory alarm devices.

Advantages:
1. Extremely flexible type of system; it may be used to protect safes, file cabinets, windows, doors, partitions; in fact, any unguarded metallic object within maximum tuning range may be protected;
2. Simple to install and operate;
3. Fully transistorized types require no AC power;
4. Provides an invisible protective field, making it difficult for intruder to determine when system has been set off;
5. High salvage value—may be easily dismantled and reinstalled;
6. Compact equipment size;
7. High grade of protection.

Disadvantages:
1. Can be applied only to ungrounded equipment;
2. "Housekeeping" of protected area or object must be carefully watched;
3. Accidental alarms can occur if protected area or object is carelessly approached, e.g., by porters or cleaners at night.

Maintenance of Intrusion-Detection Devices

Intrusion-detection devices should remain in continuous operation during nonoperational hours if they are to be effective security aids. There are situations where it may be necessary to have a continuous 24-hour operation. Therefore, preventive and corrective maintenance should be performed properly. Each device should be capable of operation from a built-in source to compensate for the vulnerability of power sources outside the installation. The time requirement for such capability must be evaluated in each case, depending upon such factors as alternate power supplies, maintenance support, hours of active operation, and so forth.

Maintenance is not a difficult problem if proper care is routinely exercised. Most malfunctions, if the device has been properly selected, installed and adjusted, result from improper maintenance. To prevent malfunctions, all component parts must be regularly inspected and tested by qualified personnel as often as recommended by manufacturers. Spare parts, such as tubes, condensers, relays, and other parts as recommended by the manufacturer, should be stocked locally.

Normally, manufacturers will train and advise your personnel on the maintenance of their equipment. To insure proper operation of detection systems:

1. Designated personnel should be available and capable of effecting immediate minor repairs, to include replacement of burned out bulbs, replacement of fuses, maintenance and replacement of the auxiliary power unit, and detection of causes for malfunctioning of the intrusion devices and alarms. All other forms of replacement parts and repairs should be provided by support maintenance personnel.

2. If an installation cannot furnish maintenance personnel, a service contract should be negotiated with the manufacturer. In either case, maintenance service should be available on a 24-hour basis.

3. Plans and diagrams showing the location and technical data of installed devices, reporting lines, and control panels, should be classified and protected accordingly.

4. The alarm receiving area should be designed to give adequate protection to monitor personnel, as this will be a prime target for an intruder. Provision for emergency assistance to this area should be

established. Appropriate measures should be employed to safeguard against collusion or detection by monitor personnel. Admittance to this area should be restricted to supervisory and maintenance personnel.

Personnel on duty at master control points at installations or facilities utilizing intrusion-detection devices should maintain a daily record of all devices including the number of alarms and any malfunctions experienced. Operational records should reflect:

1. Identity of person recording alarm signal;
2. Identity of area from which alarm signal is received;
3. Action taken in response to alarm signal received;
4. Total time required for responding personnel to arrive at the scene of an alarm;
5. Cause for alarm signal to be activated;
6. Tests of alarms;
7. Malfunctions, including nuisance alarms;
8. Servicing/maintenance of alarms and systems.

Perimeter Intrusion Detection

The primary means of perimeter protection continues to be personal observation. However, such observation is usually limited to that performed by periodic patrols. Intrusion-detection devices may be valuable as additional security aids if the perimeter requires continuous surveillance. The decision to use such devices depends upon the vulnerability and sensitivity of the protected area, the degree of protection deemed necessary, and the security aids currently in use.

Devices for Gate Protection

Usually, gates are protected by locks and intermittent patrol checks, or with security personnel on continuous duty, so intrusion-detection devices at gates are not justified. However, if the gate is used only intermittently, or if additional protection is desired for the gate portion of the perimeter fence line, some such device may be usefully employed.

Closed-circuit television, while not an alarm device in itself, is very useful in physical security operations and is frequently used to complement an alarm system. This may be accomplished by placing cameras at critical locations to provide direct visual monitoring from a vantage point. Closed-circuit television may be used on gates that are not manned continuously. This system normally consists of a television camera, monitor, and electric circuitry. The camera may be remotely controlled by the monitoring security personnel.

Normal utilization of TV on gates includes the use of a two-way communication system between the monitor panel and the gate, and an electrically operated gate lock. With this device the person at the monitor panel can be alerted on the speaker system by a person desiring to enter, converse with the person, observe him on the monitor to determine his authority to enter, and then release the gate lock. An adaptation may be added to this equipment to enable the monitor personnel to make a side-by-side comparison of a person's face with the picture on his identification badge. The use of closed-circuit television thus economizes on security personnel who would otherwise be checking identification at each active gate.

TV controls should be enclosed in metal housing and properly secured to preclude any attempted adjustment by unqualified personnel. The delay caused by the time required for the camera to warm up and be properly adjusted may be eliminated by keeping the camera in continuous operation. Normally, a videcon (picture tube, the most expensive single component) will last approximately five months in continuous operation.

The greatest problem in TV usage is the light intensity required for some cameras. This requirement must be determined and the availability of sufficient light verified before the system is purchased and installed. TV cameras are available which operate on a low light level. Their cost, however, is greater than others which require higher light levels, which poses a requirement to determine whether such higher cost is justified. Other problems which must be considered are the initial cost of the system, weather conditions that may hamper the visibility of the person making a positive identification of the individual desiring admittance, the use of forged or altered identification badges, and a forceful entry through the gate that was opened for the preceding entry.

Devices for Openings in Buildings

Electromechanical or circuit-breaker devices are normally suitable for openings in buildings. Most of these devices, however, can be rendered ineffective more easily than other detection devices. Therefore, precaution should be taken to make the circuitry as inaccessible as possible. Each device consists of a monitor panel, electrical circuitry, and triggering mechanisms consisting of metallic tape, contact switches, mesh or screen grids, mesh or wire stripping or a combination of these items.

Devices for the Interior of Buildings

A photoelectric alarm is an effective security aid for use at strategic points in hallways and rooms, particularly when the beam is criss-crossed to prevent avoidance by stepping over or crawling under the beam.

A device utilizing ultrasonic or microwave sound waves to detect motion is also an effective security aid for protecting rooms. This device basically consists of transmitters, receivers, a master control unit, monitor, and circuitry. Because it detects motion within the room, it is effective for detecting personnel who might have secreted themselves within the room during working hours when the alarm was not operational. Effort should be made to minimize the flow of air from heating units, air conditioners, and cracks in the building or any other possible source of air turbulence, as this may reduce the effectiveness of this device or cause nuisance alarms.

Audio-alarm devices may be used to detect sound or vibrations of sound caused by an attack upon the walls, ceilings, or floors of a protected structure. Audio-alarm devices will not detect structural vibrations. A microphone and amplifier are installed within the secured enclosure. The sensitivity of the device is adjusted so that ambient sounds such as those emanating from traffic will not trip the alarm. Because the device responds to all audible noises, it is best adapted to the protection of vaults or other solid walled enclosures which require a reasonable amount of force to enter.

When noise may cause problems, contact-type devices can be used in place of the regular microphones. These contact devices do not respond to airborne sounds but are very sensitive to vibrations within the wall or structure upon which they are mounted. Structural vibration detectors are not a substitute for audio detection devices, but they may complement them: this is an entirely separate principle of activation. Another method of eliminating extraneous sound when using audio alarms is the use of a "cancel microphone." The cancel microphone will filter such extraneous sound out of the system without interfering with the operation of the system.

One form of audio-alarm used quite frequently has the microphone and a preamplifier located in the protected area. In addition to receiving the alarm signal from the protected area, the guard may convert the system to a listening device through which he can monitor any sounds or voices that would indicate the presence or actions of intruders. One danger of this system is that security personnel are in a position to monitor classified conversations during operational hours. Precautionary measures must be taken in this type of operation to prevent any such monitoring.

Signal Lines

An alarm system is no better than the security of the lines that transmit the signal from the protected area to the responsible guard station. These lines must be sensitive enough to cause an alarm in the event of tampering. An alarm system may be defeated by an intruder regardless of the effectiveness of its triggering mechanism if the signal line is not functioning properly. Lines may be made ineffective by an intruder who has sufficient knowledge of electricity and the necessary equipment to adjust the resistance in the lines.

Manufacturers of the best commercial alarm equipment incorporate in their annunciator panels two relays, designated as the *underload* and *overload* relays. The purpose of the underload relay is to detect any appreciable drop in line current while the overload relay is intended to detect a substantial increase in current. However, if carefully accomplished, the line-defeating method mentioned above will not disturb either of the two relays.

Signal line tampering may be detected by assuring that a circuit has low line tolerance. For example, an alarm may operate on 20 milliamperes of line current. If the overload relay is set to drop out when the line current exceeds 30 milliamperes and the underload relay will drop out at 10 milliamperes, the line tolerance is said to be 20 milliamperes. Most standard alarm circuits have line tolerances ranging from three milliamperes (for storage vault installations) to 30 milliamperes (for many window-foil and door-switch protected rooms). Systems having line supervision on tolerance in the milliampere range can be defeated with little difficulty. To be effective, line tolerance must not exceed 25 milliamperes.

If signal lines for alarm systems installed at important facililties extend outside protected areas, they are vulnerable to tampering; where feasible, microampere line sensitivity should be provided.

The need for constant electronic or other surveillance of transmission lines must be emphasized to insure awareness of security personnel, and this is normally the weakest link in the system. Emphasis must also be placed on the necessity to maintain records of nuisance alarms, and on continuing maintenance to insure proper operation of the system at all times.

Contact Microphone System with Integration and Discrimination

The contact microphone, a system with integration and discrimination, has been designed for the protection of masonry-constructed enclosures fitted with heavy steel doors. The system is capable of detecting attempted penetration of any part of the enclosure as a result of explosion, hammering, cutting, drilling, or burning attacks. To accomplish this, the system uses contact microphones that detect vibrations sent through the structure walls by the attempted penetration. The unit contains a memory bank which can be set to record a predetermined number of blows before transmitting an alarm; this feature reduces nuisance alarms. A "bleeder unit" clears the memory bank over a specified time period. The detected vibrations are amplified and electrically integrated by a transistorized audio-amplifier which has both amplitude and frequency discrimination, and are finally transformed into an alarm signal at the guard headquarters. The amplifier is also provided with a means for listening into ambient noise in the structure walls so that unusual noises can be analyzed and identified, thus facilitating maintenance and troubleshooting. Because the contact microphones sense wall vibrations rather than airborne sounds, the system is not affected by airborne noises.

Communication Systems

Protective communication systems will vary in size and type with the importance, vulnerability, size, location, radio receptivity, and other factors affecting a specific installation. Normally, the regular communication system of an installation is not adequate for protective security purposes. Security forces should have their own communication system with direct lines outside and an auxiliary power supply. Although principal dependence is placed on the telephone, the teletype, and the automatic alarm system, interior and exterior radio communications play an important part in the protective net of large installations. One or more of the following means of communication should be included in the protective system:

1. Facilities for local exchange and commercial telephone service.

2. Intraplant, interplant, and interoffice telephone systems utilizing either government-owned or rented circuits and equipment, but not interconnected with facilities for commercial exchange or toll telephone service.

3. Radiotelephone and/or radiotelegraph facilities for either point-to-point or mobile service.

4. Telegraph and teletype facilities for either commercial service or private line operation.

5. Central station automatic alarm system.

6. Hand-carried portable radios and/or receivers, with transmitters stationed strategically throughout the installation.

7. A security supervisory system consisting of key operated electric call boxes located strategically throughout an installation. By inserting the key in the call box, security personnel can make routine tour reports or summon emergency assistance. Tampering with the transmitting key or the call box automatically locks the latter, causing a failure of the signal and an alert for immediate investigation.

Alternate Communication System

Alternate communication systems must be provided for use in emergencies. The flood of inquiries that follow emergency conditions added to the normal flow of messages may overload the existing system at the very time that sure and rapid communication systems should be separated from other communication lines, and should be in underground conduits. For emergency communication with agencies outside the installation, leased wires or a radio adjustable to civil police and fire department frequencies should be available.

Wiring, Inspection, and Testing

Whenever practicable, the wiring of protective alarm and communication systems should be on separate poles or in separate conduits from the installation communication and lighting systems. Tamper resistant wire and cable, with sheath of foil that transmits a signal when penetrated or cut, will provide added protection.

All alarm and communication circuits should be tested at least once during each shift, preferably when the new shift comes on duty. At small installations that do not employ guards, a test should be made immediately before closing for the night. Some commercially manufactured systems have self-testing features which should be checked periodically by the security patrol or operating force. All equipment must be inspected periodically by technical maintenance personnel, who will repair or replace worn or failing parts.

Lock and Key System

Locks, Keys, and Combinations

The lock is one of the basic safeguards in protecting installations, personnel, and property. All containers, rooms, buildings, and facilities containing vulnerable or sensitive items should be locked when not in use. However, regardless of their quality or cost, locks should be considered delay devices only, and not positive bars to entry. Many ingenious locks have been devised, but equally ingenious means have been developed to open them. Some types of locks require considerable time and expert manipulation for covert opening, but all will succumb to force and the proper tools.

A well-constructed vault, safe, or filing cabinet is only as secure as the resistance of the locking mechanism to picking, manipulation, or drilling. Types of locking devices include:

1. *Key Locks.* Most key locks can be picked by an expert in a few minutes. The possibility of the loss and compromise of a key and the

possibility of an impression being made should also be considered in determining the security value of a key-type lock.

2. *Conventional Combination Locks.* This type lock may be opened by a skillful manipulator, who may be able to determine the settings of the tumblers and construction of a common three-position dial-type combination lock through his senses of touch and hearing. Although the manipulation of some combination locks may require several hours, a skillful manipulator can open an average conventional combination lock in a few minutes.

3. *Manipulation-Resistant Combination Locks.* A manipulation-proof lock is so designed that the opening lever does not come in contact with the tumblers until the combination has been set. Such a lock furnishes a high degree of protection for highly-classified or important material.

4. *Other Combination Locks.* Combination locks with four or more tumblers may be desirable for containers of highly important items.

5. *Relocking Devices.* A relocking device on a safe or vault door furnishes an added degree of security against forcible entry. Such a device appreciably increases the difficulty of opening a combination lock container by means of punching, drilling, or blocking the lock or its parts. It is recommended for heavy safes and vaults.

6. *Interchangeable Cores.* The interchangeable core system utilizes a lock with a core that can be removed and replaced by another core using a different key. Its main features include:

- Cores may be quickly replaced, instantly changing the matching of locks and keys if their security is compromised.
- All locks can be keyed into an overall complete master-keyed locking system.
- Economical due to reduction in maintenance costs and new lock expense.
- System is flexible and can be engineered to the installation's needs.
- Simplifies record-keeping.

7. *Cipher Locks.* A cipher lock is a digital (push-buttons numbered from 1 through 9) combination door-locking device used to deny area access to any individual not authorized or cleared for a specific area.

Numerous locking systems are available, and others are being developed which use neither keys nor combinations. These include locks that open when a punched card is inserted; others that open when a fingerprint (previously recorded in a memory bank) is placed on a glass plate; another type opens when a previously recorded voice speaks into a microphone. The physical security officer should keep abreast of all such devices and their development, and coordinate with the engineer officer to recommend their use where appropriate.

In addition to padlocks being susceptible to manipulation and picking, there is also the danger of an identical lock with a known key or combination being substituted for a lock in use. For this reason padlocks should always be snapped shut on one of the locking eyes of a container while it is open. Some of the different designations of keys and locks are:

1. *Operating keys*—keys that are in daily use to open locks.

2. *Duplicate keys*—those which duplicate operating keys and are usually stored for use in an emergency (e.g., loss of a key or absence of the holder of the operating key). They must be stored securely in a safe or other locked container.

3. *Master keys*—those which open a series of locks. They are used only as a matter of convenience in carrying one key instead of numerous keys. They must be carefully controlled, and all markings which identify them as master keys removed. Master-keying results in an increase of susceptibility to picking it. It should be used, if at all, on the lowest level possible, to limit the possible uses of a single key.

4. *Reserve locks with keys*—those used to rotate other locks or to provide for new requirements. They must be secured in the same way as duplicate keys.

Issuance and Control of Locks and Keys

Of primary importance in the safeguarding of property or classified material is a good lock and key issuance and control system. Such a system includes control of the combinations of locks. For effective control, accurate records should be maintained and periodic physical inspections and inventories made. The main principles of this system follow.

1. Combinations or keys should be accessible only to those persons whose official duties require access to them.

2. Combinations and locks should be changed once a year or after:
   —The loss or possible compromise of the combination or key;
   —The discharge, suspension, or reassignment of any person having knowledge of the combination;
   —The receipt of a container with built-in combination lock.

3. More frequent rotation of key padlocks may be required in certain instances.

4. In selecting combination numbers, multiples and simple ascending or descending arithmetical series should be avoided.

5. When padlocks with fixed combinations are used in conjunction with bar locks as supplemental locking devices, an adequate supply should be maintained to permit frequent interchange of locks among users. This type of lock does not provide adequate security unless it is used in large numbers over extensive areas, which permits a successful interchange without compromise.

6. Records containing combinations should be placed in the same security classification as that material which the lock secures.

7. Use of keys must be based on the same general concept as applied to safe combinations. Issuance of keys must be kept to a minimum and retained under constant key control supervision. Generally the installation key system should be under the control of the installation's chief security officer. The following measures are recommended for the control of keys to magazines, trailers, warehouses, and other structures containing classified matter or highly pilferable materials.

—Keys should be stored in a locked, fireproof container when not in use.
—Access lists for persons authorized to draw keys to classified storage facilities should be maintained in the key storage container.
—Keys should not be issued for personal retention or removal from the installation.
—Key containers should be checked at the end of each shift and all keys must be accounted for.

Key control records should be maintained on all key systems. Accountability can be maintained by records, key cards, and key control registers. These records must include at least the following information:

1. Total number of keys and blanks in the system;
2. Total number of keys by each keyway code;
3. Number of keys issued;
4. Number of keys on hand;
5. Number of blanks on hand for each keyway code;
6. Persons to whom keys have been issued.

Inventories of key systems should be conducted not less often than annually. Requests for issuance of new, duplicate, or replacement keys should be approved or monitored by the official responsible for key control.

A key depository should be provided at installations where keys are secured during nonoperational hours. Supervisors should be required to sign a register for the keys at the beginning of each working day and to turn in keys at the end of the working day. Security personnel should check the key board and register to insure accountability for all keys.

Key control systems will normally be engineered to provide the degree of security required with a minimum impairment of the operational mission. Basic requirements for all key control systems are as follows:

1. High-security pin-tumbler cylinder locks should normally be specified for use.

2. Key control systems must be developed to insure against usable keys being left in possession of contractors or other unauthorized personnel. Such assurance is normally achieved by utilizing locks with restricted keyways and by issuing new keys on key blank stock that is not readily available to commercial keymakers.

3. Master-keying, when employed, should be kept to an absolute minimum. When pin-tumbler systems are master-keyed, the use of several shorter pins to facilitate two or more acceptable pin positionings reduces the security afforded by use of a maximum number of pins in a non-master-keyed lock. Utilization of one or more mushroom-type pins or a variation of this type pin should be utilized in each lock. Also, individual pins should not be segmented more than two times on those locks being used to secure more sensitive material.

4. All locks (lock cylinders when appropriate) and keys in a master-keyed system should be numbered with unrelated number systems.

Key Control Officer

A key control officer could be appointed by the chief security officer. He may be the provost marshal or the physical security officer, or other designated individual. This officer should be concerned with the supply of locks and how they are stored; the handling of keys; records maintenance; investigation of loss of keys; inventories and inspections; custody of master keys and control keys if applicable; regulations concerning locks and keys on the installation and facility; maintenance and operation of the installation's key depository; the overall supervision of the key program at the installation.

The key control officer should maintain a permanent record of the following:

1. Locks by number, showing:

—Location of each lock;
—Key combination, i.e., pin lengths and positions;
—Date of last key change.

2. Keys by number, showing:

—Location of each key;
—Type and key combination of each key;
—A record of all keys not accounted for.

The key control officer should also be responsible for procuring locks and keys. Based on determined requirements, he should coordinate procurement with the locks and keys that have proven effective.

Mechanics of Implementation

Since each installation or facility will have conditions and requirements peculiar to its activity, key control systems will vary. Before establishing a system, a survey should be conducted to determine actual requirements and to identify all warehouses, shops, storage areas, safes, filing cabinets, etc. that require the additional protection of locking devices and keys. When this determination has been made, an annex to the physical security plan can be prepared showing:

1. Location of key depositories;
2. Keys (by building, area, or cabinet number) to be turned in to each depository;
3. Method of marking or tagging keys for ready identification;
4. Method of control for issue and receipt of keys to include maintenance of registers and identification of personnel authorized possession of keys;
5. Action required in the event keys are lost, stolen, or misplaced;
6. Frequency and method of lock rotation;
7. Assignment of responsibilities by job or position title;
8. Emergency keys readily available to the security supervisor;
9. Other controls as deemed necessary.

Types and Applications of Intrusion-Detection Devices

Systems	Basis of activation	Application	Maintenance supervision problems	Nuisance alarms	Rating
Audio	Sound	Interior only (for vaults and low sound level areas).	Regular inspection to replace inoperative parts.	Frequent (from extraneous sounds).	Interior use only
Sonic	Movement	Interior only.	Same as above	Few.	More reliable than audio.
Ultrasonic	Movement	Interior only.	Same as above	Few.	More reliable for protection of rooms.
Microwave	Movement	Interior only.	Same as above	Few.	Most reliable within patterns set by antennae.
Electromechanical	Breaking of electric circuits.	Interior only (doors, windows, skylights, ventilators, etc.).	Same as above	Few (window tape may break).	Affords minimum protection for buildings and rooms.
Electromagnetic (interior)	Movement	Interior only (metal cabinets and safes).	Same as above	Few	Reliable for metal safes and cabinets.
Electromagnetic (exterior)	Movement	Exteriors only (perimeters and also can be attached to side of building).	Same as above. Also to remove snow, ice, and debris from fence.	Many	Best device developed for fence line security.
Closed circuit TV	Visual	Interior and exterior	Same as above. Also to dry lenses.	None	Very effective for remote surveillance.
Photoelectric	Interrupting light beam	Interior and exterior (rooms, halls, gates, and perimeters).	Same as above. Also to clean transmitter and receiver.	Interior (few), exterior (many) (due to fog, rain, birds, etc.).	Interior: reliable when beams are crisscrossed for short distances. Exterior: gates and short distances only.

4

Personnel Identification and Movement Control

While perimeter barriers, intrusion-detection devices, and protective lighting provide physical security safeguards, alone they are not enough. A positive personnel identification and control system must be established and maintained in order to achieve required compartmentalization, preclude unauthorized entry, and facilitate authorized entry at personnel control points. Access lists, personal recognition, security identification cards or badges, badge exchange procedures, and personnel escorts are elements that contribute to the effectiveness of identification and control systems. The best control is provided when systems incorporate all these elements. Simple, understandable, and workable identification and control measures and procedures should be utilized to achieve security objectives without impeding operations. Properly organized and administered, a personnel and movement control system provides a means not only of positively identifying those who have the right and need to enter or leave an area, but also of detecting unauthorized personnel who attempt to gain entry. These objectives are achieved by:

1. Determining who has a valid requirement to be in an area;
2. Limiting access to persons who have that valid requirement;
3. Establishing procedures for positive identification of persons within, or with authorized access into, areas;
4. Issuing special identification cards or badges to personnel authorized access into restricted areas;
5. Using access lists;
6. Using identification codes.

Additional purposes of control are to prevent the introduction of harmful devices, material, or components; and to prevent the misappropriation, pilferage, or compromise of material or recorded information.

Screening of job applicants and employees to eliminate potential security risks is important. For the results of such screening to be most effective, it is desirable that they be incorporated into standard personnel policies.

The use of a personnel security questionnaire is essential in investigating both applicants and employees. The security questionnaire should be checked for completeness and, in the case of applicants, obvious undesirables eliminated from further consideration. A careful investigation should be conducted to assure that the applicant's or employee's character, associations, and suitability for employment are satisfactory.

The following sources may be helpful in obtaining data for personnel security investigations:

1. State and local police
2. Employers
3. References (including those not furnished by applicant or employee; these are known as "throw-offs," and their names are obtained during interviews of references furnished by applicants or employees)
4. Public records
5. Credit agencies
6. Schools (all levels)

The Identification System

An identification system should be established at each installation or facility to provide a means of identification for all security personnel, employees, and visitors. The system should provide for the use of security identification cards or badges to aid in the control and movement of personnel into, within, and out of specified areas or activities. The identification card or badge should be designed as simply as possible and still provide adequate identification for controlling the movement of personnel.

The provisions for identification by card or badge at an installation or facility should be included as part of the physical security plan. The following should be prescribed.

1. Designation of the various areas where identification cards and badges are required;
2. Description of the various identification media in use and the authorization and limitations placed upon the holder;
3. Mechanics of identification when entering and leaving each area, including nonoperational hours;

4. Details of where, when, and how badges should be worn or cards displayed;
5. Procedures to follow in case of loss or damage to identification media;
6. Procedures for the disposition of identification media on termination of employment or as a result of security investigations and flagging actions;
7. A procedure to reissue new identification media when one to five percent, depending on the type of security (restricted) area to which the badge gives access, have been lost or are unaccounted for.

Access List

Admission to restricted areas should be granted only to those persons who are positively identified and whose names appear on a properly authenticated access list of all persons authorized to enter. Each time a permanent addition or deletion is made, a new access list should be prepared and the old list destroyed.

Escorts

At a restricted installation or facility, or at a restricted area *within* an unrestricted installation or facility, a person whose name is not on the access list must be escorted from the entrance to his destination. Whether or not the escort remains with such visitor during the time he is within the restricted area is determined by regulations.

Personnel Recognition System

A personal recognition system is the surest method of establishing positive identification. This system may be used in conjunction with an access list to admit and control the movement of installation or facility personnel within a restricted area employing less than 30 persons per shift who are known to the security personnel personally and are subject to a low rate of turnover. In those areas where large groups of personnel are admitted at once, personal recognition also may be used. This is done by having personnel enter and exit the area in a group under the supervision of a responsible individual who personally identifies all members of the group to the security force.

Card and Badge Systems

A security identification card or badge system should be established to admit and control the movement of all persons in restricted areas employing 30 or more persons per shift. However, the chief security officer may want to authorize a card or badge system in restricted areas where less than 30 persons per shift are employed. Of the several identification systems used in access control, three of the most common are the single card or badge system, the card or badge exchange system, and the multiple card or badge system. These identification systems involve either cards carried on the person, cards or badges worn on the outer apparel, or issuance of identification cards or badges at the main entrance to an installation.

Single Card or Badge System. With a single card or badge system, permission to enter different areas is shown by letters, numerals, or colors. For instance, blue may be the current designated background color for general admittance to an installation. Permission to enter specific areas of higher restriction within the installation may be designated by specified symbols or colors overprinted on the card or badge. This system gives comparatively loose control and is not recommended for security areas. Permission to enter is not always analogous with the "need to know," and the fact that identification cards and badges frequently remain in the bearer's possession during off-duty or off-post hours gives the opportunity for surreptitious alteration or duplication.

Card or Badge Exchange System. This is a system of two cards or badges containing identical photographs but having different background colors, or an overprint on one of the two. One type is presented at the entrance and exchanged for the other, which is carried or worn while within the area. This second is identical in every way except for additional symbols or colors which grant further admittance. The Polaroid camera with a special adaptor can make up to four prints for one picture. This method provides extra security by having both photographs identical. In this system the second badge or card is kept in the security area and never leaves the area, thus decreasing the possibility of forgery or alteration.

Multiple Card or Badge System. This is a further development of the exchange system. Instead of having specific markings on the identification card or badge denoting permission to enter various restricted areas, an exchange is made at the entrance to each security area. Exchange cards or badges are kept at each area for only those individuals who have the appropriate card or badge. By virtue of the localized and controlled exchange requirements, this is the most secure and effective system.

Identification Card and Badge Specifications

Security identification cards and badges should be designed and constructed to be tamperproof. Security identification card and badge inserts should be prenumbered to avoid the possibility of reissuing any number.

Since any identification card or badge may be altered or reproduced by a person having the time and sufficient skill in printing, engraving and photocopying, the makeup, issuance, and accountability of cards and badges must be fully controlled. This control commences with the manufacturer or supplier. When inserts or complete cards or badges are secured commercially, verification should be made that adequate control is exercised by the supplier. This is especially important where an engraving or a special paper is concerned.

Identification card or badge issuance, accountability, and control should be administered from a central office, preferably the office of the physical security officer, so that minimum time elapses between a change in the status of a card or badge and the notification of the security forces. A duplicate of each issued card or badge and a file on each bearer should be kept, including, in addition to the data entered on the card or badge, the bearer's residential address and telephone number. Strict control must be exercised to insure the return and destruction of cards and badges on termination of assignment or employment of personnel, and invalidate those lost or mutilated.

Enforcement Measures

Enforcement is the most vulnerable link in any identification system. Perfunctory performance of duty by the security forces in comparing the bearer with the card or badge may weaken or destroy the effects of the most elaborate system. Positive enforcement measures should be prescribed to insure effective operation of the identification system. These should include:

1. Security personnel designated for duty at entrance control points; personnel should be chosen for their alertness, tact, and good judgment.

2. A uniform method of handling or wearing security identification cards or badges. If carried on the person, the card must be removed from the wallet or other container and handed to security personnel. A badge should be worn in a conspicuous position to expedite inspection and recognition from a distance.

3. Entrances and exits of restricted areas, so arranged that arriving and departing personnel are forced to pass in a single file in front of the security personnel. In some instances the use of turnstiles may be advisable to assist in maintaining positive control of entrance and exit.

4. Artificial lighting at the control points, so arranged that it illuminates the arriving and departing personnel; lighting should be of sufficient intensity to enable the security personnel to compare and identify the bearer with the identification card or badge.

5. Positioning of identification card and badge racks or containers at control points for an exchange system so that they are accessible to guard personnel only.

6. Maintenance of an accurate written record or log listing, by serial number, all cards and badges showing those on hand, to whom issued, and disposition (lost, mutilated, or destroyed).

7. Authentication of records and logs by the custodian.

8. Periodic inventory of records.

9. Prompt invalidation of lost cards and badges.

10. Conspicuous posting at security control points of current lists of lost or invalidated cards and badges.

11. Establishment of controls within restricted areas to enable the security personnel to determine promptly and accurately the number of persons within the area at any time.

12. Establishment of procedures to control movement of visitors to security areas. A visitor control record should be maintained and located where positive controls can be exercised.

The Two-Man Rule

The two-man rule requires, for reasons of safety and security, the presence of at least two authorized persons, each capable of detecting incorrect procedures with respect to the task to be performed, and each familiar with pertinent safety and security requirements.

This rule should not be considered as applicable only in the cited situations; it should be applied in many other aspects of physical security operations, such as the following:

1. Where uncontrolled access to vital equipment or material might provide opportunity for intentional or unintentional damage which could affect the mission or operation of the installation or facility;

2. Where uncontrolled access to funds could provide opportunity for diversion by falsification of accounts;

3. Where uncontrolled delivery or receipt for materials could provide opportunity for pilferage through "short" deliveries and false receipts.

Visitor Identification and Control

For security purposes, the term "visitor" means any person (including installation or facility personnel) not listed on the permanent access list for the area being visited.

Physical security precaution against pilferage and sabotage requires screening, identification, and control of visitors. Visitors can be categorized generally:

1. Persons with whom every installation or facility must have dealings in the conduct of its business; e.g., representatives of suppliers, customers, licensors or licensees, insurance inspectors or adjusters, government

inspectors (national, state, and local), service industry representatives, contractors, employees, etc.

2. Individuals or groups who visit an installation or facility for a purpose not essential to, or necessarily in furtherance of, the operations of the installation or facility concerned. Such visits may be by business, educational, technical or scientific organizations and individuals or groups desiring to further their particular interest.

3. Guided tour visits to selected portions of installations in the interest of public relations.

Arrangements for the identification and control of visitors may include:

1. Positive methods of establishing the authority for admission of visitors, as well as any limitations relative to access.

2. Positive identification of visitors by means of personal recognition, visitor permit, or other identifying credentials. The employee, supervisor, or officer in charge should be contacted to ascertain the validity of the visit.

3. Availability and use of visitor registration forms and records which will provide a record of identity of the visitor, time and duration of his visit, and other pertinent control data.

4. Availability and use of visitor identification cards or badges. Such identification media should be numbered serially and should indicate the following:

—Bearer's name
—Area or areas to which access is authorized
—Escort requirements, if any
—Time limit
—Signature (or facsimile)
—Photograph, if desired and available

5. Procedures which will insure supporting personal identification in addition to check of visitor cards or badges at restricted area entrances.

6. Procedures for escorting visitors through areas where an uncontrolled visitor, even though conspicuously identified, could acquire information for which he is not authorized.

7. Controls which will recover visitor identification cards or badges on expiration, or when no longer required.

8. Twenty-four-hour advance approval when possible. Where appropriate, management should prepare an agenda for the visit and designate an escort.

Enforcement of access control systems rests primarily on the installation security forces; however, it is essential that they have the full cooperation of the employees, who should be educated and encouraged to assume this security responsibility. Employees should be instructed to consider each unidentified or improperly identified individual as a trespasser. In restricted areas where access is limited to particular zones, employees should report movement of individuals to unauthorized zones.

Contractor Employees

Contractors usually know their key personnel, but frequently the bulk of their employees are transient laborers who are comparatively unknown to their employer. In a construction project involving a considerable number of men over a long period of time, it is advisable to fence off the construction area from the rest of the installation. Where the contract work is infrequent and for comparatively short periods of time, security surveillance may be more economical. Each instance will have to be considered separately, based on the physical layout and the sensitivity of the installation. It is advisable to make at least local background checks on contractor personnel.

Utility and Maintenance Personnel

No guise has been used more successfully and more often as the "cover" for unauthorized entry than that of service and maintenance personnel. Appropriate clothing, a tool box, and a smattering of technical knowledge are the only requirements to pose as a telephone repairman, an electrician, a plumber, or a business machine maintenance man. Legitimate employees of public utilities and some commercial service organizations usually carry company identification; however, they should not be admitted to a restricted area without at least a telephone check with their office to establish their authenticity and without a check with the person who supposedly requested the service. Movement within the installation or facility should be subject to the same identification and escort procedures as prescribed for other visitors during duty or off-duty hours. Full-time maintenance personnel may be accredited in the same manner as other employees.

Control of Movement of Employees After Hours

A system should be maintained for the control of personnel who remain within the installation or facility after normal hours, whereby the security force can record their departure time. In many cases the individual may have a valid reason for staying late; however, he may be concerned with some illegal activity which is not readily apparent. By recording name, departure time, and identification card or badge number, a permanent record can be established and the individual can be questioned at a later time if necessary. Personnel should not be allowed to enter a restricted area outside of normal duty hours without special authorization. This authorization can be in written form, or given verbally by officially designated individuals.

Package Control

A good package control system is an invaluable aid in helping to prevent or minimize pilferage or sabotage. No packages should be brought into restricted areas without inspection.

A positive system should be established to control movement of packages, material, and property into and out of the installation. Limitations as to types of property authorized, persons allowed to move authorized property, and approved points of entrance and exit should be included in the installation physical security plan.

When practicable, all out-going packages should be inspected except those properly authorized for removal. When 100 percent inspection is impracticable, frequent unannounced spot checks should be conducted. Property controls must not be limited to packages carried openly, but must include controls of articles of clothing, handbags, briefcases, umbrellas, lunch boxes, and anything of a similar nature which may be used to conceal property or material of any type.

Registration of Vehicles

Vehicles Privately Owned and Operated. All motor vehicles privately owned and operated by personnel should be registered with the physical security office and should be required to display a tag or decal. Prerequisites for registration normally include:

1. Evidence of ownership and a state certificate of registration;
2. Valid operator's license or permit issued by the state in which the vehicle is registered;
3. Motor vehicle liability insurance;
4. Vehicle inspection (where deemed necessary by the commander);
5. Issuance of a decal.

Additional Procedure. Such vehicle registration and display of a decal does not excuse the driver from compliance with the normal personal identification and admittance procedures.

Registration of Visitors' Vehicles. All visitors' vehicles should be registered. Registration should include the make of vehicle, license number, name of driver, destination, purpose of visit, and time and date of entry and departure. These vehicles should be identified by a temporary decal or identification medium different from permanent registrations to permit ready recognition. Visitors should be directed to specifically designated parking areas. Where visitors are permitted entry to an installation after normal duty hours, local regulations normally specify the conditions of entry and other limitations to assure proper control at all times.

Temporary Registration. At some installations and facilities, especially where there is a considerable turnover of permanent personnel, it is advisable to issue a temporary registration, valid for 72 hours, to permit sufficient time for personnel to comply with the permanent registration procedure or to clear the installation or facility after permanent registration has been cancelled.

Tags and Decals. State laws differ as to the type and placement permitted for other than state registration tags, so check the applicable laws before planning such measures.

Vehicle Parking Control

Parking areas for privately owned vehicles should be located outside the perimeter of protected areas. Parking areas should be fenced and lighted. Entrances and exits to parking areas should be separate from others. The method of parking should be clearly marked and strictly enforced.

If all cars cannot be parked outside restricted areas, only employees should be allowed to park within the enclosure. When interior parking is unavoidable, the parking area should be located away from important facilities or processes, and separately fenced in so that occupants of automobiles must pass through a pedestrian gate before entering the facility. To prevent unauthorized removal of property, security personnel should monitor movements of personnel to parking areas.

Sufficient parking space should be provided for visitors near access control points to prevent them from entering areas other than those necessary. Visitors parking areas should be under close scrutiny to prevent unauthorized removal of property.

Truck Control

All trucks entering or leaving should be closely inspected. An orderly system should be established to limit and control the movement of trucks and other conveyances within such areas. Where possible, loading and unloading platforms should be located outside protected areas. If this is not possible, turnaround areas for loading and unloading should be at or as near as possible to the truck gates. This will help to eliminate irregularities by dishonest employees and truckers during shipment loading and unloading.

All trucks and conveyances entering or leaving a protected area should be required to pass through a service gate manned by security personnel. Truck drivers, helpers, passengers, and vehicle contents should be carefully examined. The security check at truck entrances should cover both incoming and outgoing trucks and should include:

1. Appropriate entries on a truck register, including registration of truck owner, signatures of driver and helper, description of load, and date and time of entrance and departure.
2. Identification of driver and helper, including proof of affiliation with the company owning the truck or conveyance.
3. A license check of the vehicle operator and his driver or helper.
4. Examination of the truck or conveyance for unauthorized items, if feasible.

Identification cards or badges should be issued to truck drivers and helpers who have been properly identified and registered. Such cards or badges should permit access only to specific loading and unloading areas.

Incoming trucks should be kept to the minimum essential for the efficient operation of the installation, and escorts must be provided whenever vehicles, commercial or government, are permitted to enter designated "limited" or "exclusion" areas.

For trucks with loads that are impractical to examine, door seals may be used on incoming vehicles by the security personnel at the entrance gate. These seals will be opened by a designated representative at the receiving end. Likewise, the truck doors may be resealed for exit or other stops within the installation.

Loading and unloading operations should be strictly supervised by security forces to assure that unauthorized materiel or persons do not enter or leave the installation via trucks or other conveyances. Trash details working in restricted areas should be supervised by security personnel.

Petroleum products, especially those delivered under commercial contracts, require special security measures to prevent pilferage or diversion of the bulk product.

1. The best preventive measure is verification, at the loading point, of the amount loaded, and verification of the amount discharged at the delivery point. Any discrepancy should be immediately reported and investigated.
2. Locks and/or seals may be used to secure container covers after loading. These should be inspected on departure from the loading point and on arrival at the delivery point to insure that they have not been tampered with. Seal numbers must be checked against the numbers shown on the waybill.

3. Frequent checks of the locks and seals, as well as the route of travel to preclude unauthorized "detours," will assist the preventive effort.

4. All personnel should be alert for any indication of a modification to the delivery vehicle that permits retaining a portion of the load in an apparently empty tank. Any such indication should be thoroughly checked out.

Railroad Car Control

The movement of railroad cars should be supervised, and the cars inspected, to prevent the entry or removal of unauthorized personnel or materiel. Inspecting personnel should be especially watchful for explosives or incendiaries.

All railroad entrances should be controlled by locked gates when not in use, and should be under security supervision when unlocked or opened for passage of railroad cars. Ideally, railroad car loading and unloading platforms should be located outside restricted areas.

Railroad switching should be confined to daylight hours if it does not materially interfere with the efficiency of operations.

The number of the seals on all sealed railroad cars should be checked, immediately upon arrival at the installation, against the list of seal numbers (which should be requested from the shipper). Broken seals or seal numbers not in accordance with the list from the shipper warrant immediate investigation.

5

Storage Security

A storage area may be a warehouse, a shed, an open area, or any portion of an installation which is used for storage. The general security considerations for installations and facilities set forth in this manual apply to storage areas.

In planning measures for the security of supplies in storage, the nature of the material stored, the geography of the area, economic considerations, and anything else peculiar to the situation must be considered.

While the responsibility of the physical security officer is the security, and not the operations, of the depot, he can discharge his responsibilities fully only if he becomes familiar with the general methods and techniques of depot and storage operations. Following are some specialized terms used in such operations.

Storage Space: Any space, without regard to type of construction or improvement, used for storage.

Storage Building: Any building constructed or acquired for the storage of supplies, even though some part of it has been diverted to and is used for offices, depot utility storage or repair shops. Depot utility storage buildings, except when they are in whole or in part for the storage of supplies, are not considered storage buildings. The actual area used for storage purposes within such a building is considered storage space for reporting purposes.

Warehouse Space: Area in a building designed for storage purposes and constructed with roof and complete side and end walls.

Heated Space: Area in which the temperature may be controlled by the application of heat within specified limits.

Unheated Space: Area not equipped with heating facilities.

Humidity-Controlled Space: Warehouse area equipped with humidity-control equipment.

Flammable Space: Warehouse area designed for the storage of highly flammable material.

Shed Space: Space in a covered structure having one or more sides or ends open or both.

Other Space: Space used for storage in a structure designed for purposes other than storage (e.g., dry tanks, hangars, transitory shelters).

Gross Space: Inside area between exterior walls without deductions for fire walls and other structural losses. Overall measurements of open storage area with no deductions for trackage and permanent roads in the area.

Bin Storage: Storage of unpackaged parts, subassemblies, assemblies, or end items in bins so that an item may be withdrawn without breaking open a package containing a number of such items.

Aisle in Storage Space: Any passage within a storage area.

Receiving and Shipping Space: Gross space designated as work area for receipt and shipment of supplies and equipment.

Non-storage Space: That area within gross space that is not used for storage because of structural losses or designation for purposes other than storage. Includes transit shed space when used or reserved for that purpose.

Net Storage Space: The floor area on which bins are erected plus the floor area on which material can be stored.

Open Storage Space: Ground area designated for storage.

Open Improved Storage Space: Open area that has been graded and that has a hard surface prepared with topping of some suitable material to permit effective materials-handling operations.

Open Unimproved Storage Space: Open area that has not been surfaced for storage purposes.

Open Unimproved Wet Space: Water area specifically allotted to and usable for the storage of floating equipment.

Tank Storage Space: Space in tanks designated for the storage of supplies other than petroleum products.

Toxic Material Open Space: Area specially prepared for storage of toxic material. For reporting purposes, it does not include the surrounding restricted area for storage because of safety-distance factors. It does include barricades and improvised coverings.

Cold Storage Warehouse: Space in which a controlled temperature below 50°F may be maintained.

Chill Space: Refrigerated warehouse space in which the temperature can be controlled between 32 and 50°F.

Freeze Space: Refrigerated warehouse area in which the temperature can be controlled below a level of 32°F.

Allocated Space: That area designated as the gross area formally apportioned for use.

Dispersed Storage Area: That portion of a depot or subinstallation located away from the main establishment but not at another reporting installation.

Site Area: In *covered storage,* the total land area required for buildings, spaced at minimum distances, plus all the necessary operating areas such as access roads, depot roads, railway sidings, and truck parks. In *open storage,* the total land surface required for net usable general storage area as defined above plus that additional area required to meet safety regulations and to operate the storage facility as a whole.

Vertical Space Occupancy Effectiveness: A factor obtained by dividing actual by potential storage height for a specific supply category.

Open Storage

Open storage is normally used only for those items of supply not subject to damage by weather conditions, and for bulky, nonperishable items not easily pilfered or disposed of. Open storage may include classified items. Both open and covered storage are vulnerable to all types of sabotage.

When property is stored in open areas, it should be properly stacked and placed within, away from, and parallel to fences in order to permit guards an unobstructed view of the fences. Stacks and lines of equipment should be a minimum of 50 feet from the perimeter barrier. They should be as symmetrical as possible, and the aisles between stacks or lines should be wide and straight. These arrangements provide good visibility for security forces. Wide fire lanes between subareas provide additional security. Early coordination between the physical security officer and the storage officer will assure proper area layout and assist in security operations.

Fixed position lights in a storage area should be of a diffused type to eliminate deep shadows. Each security patrol should be furnished with a flashlight.

Covered Storage

The same principles of even stacking and adequate aisle space recommended for use in open storage are applicable to covered storage. In case of stockpile storage where stored items are infrequently moved, the stacks may be placed to conform with existing lighting, or the lighting may be arranged after the stacks are in place. The objective is to reduce deeply shadowed areas to a minimum.

In warehouses where the stored items are moved frequently, more emphasis should be placed on security forces than upon structural or mechanical protection, especially during working hours, to prevent pilferage or sabotage by workers.

Sensitive items in storage should be kept separate from other materiel. Sensitive items are those that can be pilfered and disposed of easily, such as drugs, radio tubes, and similar items. The most satisfactory method is to store such items in a separate building with a higher degree of physical protection than other buildings. Where a separate building is not available, or where its use is not warranted by the quantity of sensitive storage, a room, cage, or crib may be constructed within a warehouse building. The floor and roof of such an enclosure must be as strong as its walls.

At an issue warehouse, back-to-back storage bins and a counter separating the issue from receiving personnel will assist in preventing pilferage.

Use of Sentry Dogs

Sentry dogs are especially valuable in storage security operations. They may be used either on-leash, as in perimeter patrol, or permitted to roam free within completely fenced-in areas. They may also be locked in a warehouse or other storage building during nonoperational hours.

Fire Prevention

The physical security officer must give consideration to fire prevention in all of his planning and operations. He must be fully aware of the details of the fire plan, and must be alert to detect and report any deficiencies. He must provide training for all security personnel on all provisions of the fire plan and their fire prevention and protection responsibilities.

6

Bomb Threats

Bomb threats, or "bomb scares," have become more frequent in recent years, paralleling increases in civil disturbances and the general rise of terrorism as a means to some political or social end.

But there are many more motives for bomb scares: Excitement may make a dull day interesting. School classes or examinations may be avoided. Airplane flights may be delayed if a passenger is late. A chance of publicity or money for reporting information may cause a person to make his own news.

The common question is, What percentage of calls actually result in bombs being found? This depends on the circumstances; however, five out of ten will call the police, even if their bomb misfires or is a dud. This may be done to prevent innocent people from being injured. In other instances an anonymous call may be received so that police and victims will not be present if a bomb does explode.

A bomb scare ties up policemen and firemen who may be needed elsewhere in emergencies. The bomb may be reported so crimes can be committed elsewhere in that patrol zone.

While there is no foolproof method of preventing such threats, or preventing their execution, the physical security measures and procedures previously discussed will assist in lessening their chances of success. In times of disturbance or unrest, or on any other indication of dissidence or dissatisfaction, control measures should be intensified.

Especially important are personnel identification and control and package and materiel control. All building occupants, security, and maintenance personnel should be alert for persons who look or act suspiciously. All personnel should be alert to observe and report suspicious objects, items or parcels which do not appear to belong in the area where they are observed. Security and maintenance personnel should make periodic checks of all rest rooms, stairwells, areas under stairwells, and other areas of the building to assure that unauthorized personnel are not in hiding in or surveying these areas.

It is also extremely important that doors be securely locked when not in use, to restrict the access of unauthorized personnel. Doors to utility closets, boiler rooms, fan rooms, telephone wire closets and switchboards, and elevator machinery rooms are especially vulnerable. Keys must be readily available in the event a search is necessary.

Handling Bomb Threats

Bomb threats may be received either by telephone or by written message. In either case, the immediate question arises as to whether the threat is genuine; that is, whether a bomb has actually been placed, or whether it is false, made only to cause a disturbance or diversion. There are many of both. In some instances bomb threats have been made by persons who intend only to cause damage to property or equipment and do not want to cause death or injury to personnel.

The first decision is whether to evacuate the threatened building(s) or area(s) and to shut down utilities such as gas and electricity. Consideration must be given to special situations, such as hospitals where evacuation of patients may be impracticable or undesirable unless the presence of a bomb is confirmed. Also, the availability of electricity or water may be necessary for the operation of medical apparati essential to the health of a patient.

The next important decision is whether to annonce a bomb threat or not; for example, in a public place, such as a school, such a public announcement may well result in a panic, with resultant injuries to persons. A consideration here is to make the announcement in a code known only to selected personnel, or to disguise the evacuation as a practice fire drill. The latter method is recommended. (Note: In a fire situation it is normal to close all doors and windows to delay spread of the fire; in a bomb situation it is better to leave all doors and windows open to dissipate the explosive force.)

Telephone Threats

Efforts should be made with the appropriate telephone officials to undertake tracing upon notification to a specific designated number. Recorders attached to telephones will be extremely helpful for later playbacks and for use in making voice prints for possible identification of the caller. In the event a bomb threat call is received, the recorder should be operated continually for a period of 24 hours following; in some instances callers have called more than once.

Persons likely to receive such a call should be briefed, and trained as necessary, in the following procedures:

1. Attempt to keep the caller on the line as long as possible, to permit tracing and to gather further information.

2. Record, in writing or by recorder, the exact words of the caller. Attempt to ascertain the location of the bomb, type of device, what it looks like, and expected time of detonation.
3. Attempt to determine the sex, the approximate age, and the attitude of the caller; specifically, any reasons or motives for his actions in placing the bomb.
4. Note any background noise, which may provide a clue to the caller's location.
5. Note any accent or peculiarity of speech which may help to identify the caller.
6. If time permits, ask the caller a question such as, Who is this calling, please? or, What is your name? In some instances, the caller may unthinkingly reply.

The items listed may be placed on a locally-devised form, to provide a checklist and easy means of recording information. In appropriate situations, such forms may be distributed to all personnel likely to receive such calls, so that they are familiar with them and are instructed in their use. A sample form, which may be adapted as appropriate, is included at the end of this chapter.

The recipient of a bomb call should be interviewed, as soon as possible following the call, by a competent interviewer. In addition to any information reported, many persons will later recall, under questioning, things they momentarily forgot, perhaps due to the stress of the incident. Such questioning must be patient and quiet, and designed only to supplement or expand on the reported information.

Written Threats

Written threats should not even be touched, if possible, since examination by trained investigators and laboratory personnel may reveal fingerprints and/or provide clues to the writer by examination of his handwriting. Excessive handling reduces, or may preclude, successful examination. The entire message, including the envelope, if any, should be preserved until released to the investigator.

Standing Operating Procedure

Each installation should have an established Standing Operating Procedure (SOP) for handling bomb threats. The SOP should be thoroughly coordinated with all concerned staff elements and agencies of the installation, and widely distributed within the installation. All personnel should be thoroughly familiar with the procedures it prescribes, and trained as appropriate.

The SOP should provide for immediate notification of appropriate personnel. A notification list, with telephone numbers, should be readily available to each possible recipient of a threat.

Occupants and the appointed custodians of threatened buildings should be notified. Depending on the physical configuration of the area, it may be necessary or advisable to notify occupants of adjacent buildings. *Radios must not be used within 150 feet of the threatened area or building, since radio waves may detonate the bomb.* SOP should provide that sirens on police, fire, and medical vehicles will not be used, since their vibrations may also detonate a bomb.

The SOP may also provide for the organization and training of evacuation units, consisting of key personnel of each building or area. The evacuation unit should be trained in the specifics of evacuating the building under conditions of a bomb threat. One consideration is priority of evacuation, i.e., evacuation by floor level. Evacuate the floor levels above the danger area in order to remove those personnel from extreme danger as quickly as possible. Training in this type of evacuation should be available from police, fire or other units within the community with such a training capability.

In the event a search is necessary, security personnel must have floor plans availabile for each building on the installation. The SOP must contain provisions that keys to locked areas, closets, utility rooms, and so forth, will be readily available to search teams. Such keys must be marked, or tagged, to indicate the locks they will open, tied in with floor plans.

SOP should provide for obtaining photographers to photograph any crowd which gathers at a scene of a bombing. Bombers frequently are drawn to the scenes of their bombings; photographs of individuals who appear repeatedly, or in more than one place, may assist in their identification.

Searching for a Bomb

To be proficient in searching the building, one must be thoroughly familiar with all hallways, rest rooms, false ceiling areas and every conceivable location in the building where an explosive or incendiary device might be concealed. When the police or fire departments arrive at the building, if they have not previously reconnoitered the building, the contents and the layout will be strange to them. Thus, it is extremely important to have a floor plan of the building.

Strange or suspicious objects should not be touched. Their location and description should be reported to the person designated to receive this information. If the danger zone is identified or located, the area should be blocked off or barricaded with a clear zone of 220 yards until the object has been removed or disarmed or until danger has passed. During a

Figure 11. A typical homemade bomb. When searching for a bomb, radios must never be used since radio waves can detonate certain kinds of bombs. (From P. Fuqua and J. Wilson, *Terrorism—The Executive's Guide to Survival,* Gulf Publishing Co., 1977.)

building search a rapid two-way communication system is of utmost importance. Such a system can be readily established through the use of existing telephones. (Do not use radios.) Medical personnel should be alerted to stand by in the event of an accident involving an explosion of the device.

The manner of searching a building varies. Advantages of occupants searching are their knowledge of the area and of the objects within it; they can conduct the search more quickly. They also have keys to locked closets and doors. If police are utilized for a search, they must leave their patrol zones to be covered by other units. Firemen are better than police for searching because they are on stand-by at the firehouse if not on a call. Their ladders, tools, lights, and other equipment may be needed for inaccessible places. Bomb squad personnel cannot quickly search large areas by themselves, but they stand by for technical advice or until an object is found. The official in charge of the search should go over a floor plan of the building with the custodian and make search assignments to insure a complete search without duplication of effort. Teams of one occupant and one fireman often work well. As a general rule, search areas should be limited to a size which can reasonably be searched in not more than 20 minutes.

During the inspection of the building, particular attention should be given to such areas as elevator shafts, ceilings (particulary rest rooms), access doors, and crawl space in rest rooms and other areas which are used as a means of immediate access to plumbing fixtures, electrical fixtures, and the like; utility and other closets; areas under stairwells; boiler and furnace rooms; flammable materials storage space; main switches and valves, e.g., electricity, gas, and fuel; indoor trash receptacles, record storage and mail rooms; ceiling lights with easily removable panels; and fire hose racks. While this list of areas to be noted with particular emphasis is not complete, it is sufficient to provide an idea of those areas where a time-delayed explosive or an incendiary device might be concealed.

Only the most obvious places can be searched in a reasonable time. A bomb may be hidden between walls or buried among numerous containers, making a complete search impossible. When a search is completed, the custodian should be told that after a thorough search a bomb was not found. Never advise that it is perfectly safe or that there is no bomb.

For a thorough description of the chemistry and mechanisms of explosives, and a close look at what executives should know about their own susceptibility to terrorist acts such as letter bombs, kidnapping, etc., see *Terrorism—The Executive's Guide to Survival,* by Paul Fuqua and Jerry Wilson, Gulf Publishing Co., 1977.

Bomb Threat Report Form

INSTRUCTIONS: Be calm. Be courteous. Listen, do not interrupt the caller.
Notify supervisor/security officer by prearranged signal while caller is on line.

Date: _____   Time: _____

Exact Words of Person Placing Call:

QUESTIONS TO ASK:

1. When is the bomb going to explode?
2. Where is the bomb right now?
3. What kind of a bomb is it?
4. What does it look like?
5. Why did you place the bomb?

TRY TO DETERMINE THE FOLLOWING (Circle as appropriate):

Caller's Identity: male   female   adult   juvenile   age

Voice: loud   soft   high pitch   deep   raspy   pleasant   intoxicated

     other

Accent: local   not local   foreign   region

Speech: fast   slow   distinct   distorted   stutter   nasal   slurred   lisp

Language: excellent   good   fair   poor   foul   other

Manner: calm   angry   rational   irrational   coherent   incoherent

     deliberate   emotional   righteous   laughing   intoxicated

Background Noises: office machines   factory machines   bedlam   trains

              animals   music   quiet   voices   mixed   airplanes

              street traffic   party atmosphere

ADDITIONAL INFORMATION:

ACTION TO TAKE IMMEDIATELY AFTER CALL: Notify your supervisor/
security officer as instructed. Talk to no one other than instructed by your super-
visor/security officer.

Receiving telephone number   **Person receiving call**

7

Physical Security Planning

The size complexity of today's industrial installations make it mandatory that security be based on a thoughtful and continuing examination of existing protective measures and a careful evaluation of the steps necessary and practicable to maintain security at the desired level.

The security plan for each installation or activity should be tailored to its security needs and local conditions. The basic element of each security plan is an armed security guard force of sufficient strength to insure the positive functioning and enforcement of established security measures and procedures. Aids and adjuncts to armed guards, such as barriers, protective lighting, intrusion-detection systems, guard communications, sentry dogs, and other measures, may be incorporated in security plans to increase the effectiveness of security forces. These must be organized in depth, and be mutually supporting, to reduce gaps in security. Selection of security measures beyond the minimum required by command directives is properly a matter of the judgment of security planners and engineers working in close coordination and cooperation.

The security plan must be formulated and implemented from a "total system" approach, that is, the plan must consider all forces performing a mission of physical security. These would include all types of interior and exterior guards.

Formulating the Physical Security Plan

This plan must provide for proper and economical utilization of personnel, must be flexible to permit timely changes for meeting emergencies, and should contain the following:

1. Purpose and objectives of the plan.
2. Area security, to include definition of areas considered critical and establishment of priorities for their protection.

3. Access control, to include establishing restrictions on access and movement into security areas; i.e., personnel access, identification and control; materiel control; vehicle control; and key control.
4. Mechanical aids to security, to include perimeter barriers, protective lighting systems, intrusion-detection systems, and communications.
5. The security force organization, with general instructions applying to all guards. Detailed instructions such as special orders and SOP should be attached as annexes.
6. Emergency actions of general application. Detailed plans for disaster and fire should be attached as annexes.

The plan should develop defense in depth where it is required. Such defense may be achieved by compartmentalization according to physical layout and/or function of subareas and implementing security measures for each, after consideration of

1. Sabotage targets
2. Pilferage targets
3. Conflicts with operations
4. Budgetary limitations

A sound physical security program is the result of good advance planning. To achieve adequate protection for an entire installation, it is necessary to prepare a detailed and timely plan which will utilize available resources in the most efficient manner.

In the plan the security officer must give primary consideration to operating requirements. In determining the type and extent of physical protection required at an installation, the following pertinent factors should be taken into consideration, in the indicated sequence:

1. A definition and a thorough analysis of the area to be protected, including the nature and arrangement of the activity; classification of information, data, activities; the number of personnel involved; monetary and/or strategic value of materiel located therein; or other salient features inherent to the problem, such as existing hazards, either natural or manmade.

2. The criticality and vulnerability of information or materiel to compromise, damage, or theft.

3. Operating, maintenance, and other requirements which must be integrated in the security plan.

4. Environment; e.g., political and economical aspects, legal considerations, terrain, climate, etc.

5. The cost of installing security equipment as well as availability of funds to provide at least minimum protection for all critical areas and activities. This minimum may be far less than the desirable degree of

physical protection; thus the plan must be flexible so that refinements can be added as additional resources become available.

6. Possible expansion, relocation, and other changes in operation. Coordination must be maintained with appropriate staff officers so that any such changes may be projected as far in advance as possible, and necessary supplemental personnel and/or funds can be obtained.

7. The feasibility, effectiveness, cost and desirability of other possible methods for providing adequate protection.

Changes in mission and activities of an installation or facility also require that the security officer make adjustments in security plans. Physical security program planning must be a continuing process if security officers are to provide the best protection possible.

All planned security measures must be employed so that they complement and supplement each other. Lack of integration of security measures may well result in a waste of money, equipment, and manpower; more important, the security of an installation may be placed in jeopardy.

Disaster Planning

In addition to the physical security provided by the protective measures discussed in preceding chapters, each installation should have an emergency plan to minimize the effects of a disaster resulting from natural or man-made causes. This plan should provide for the entire strength of the installation to engage in joint action to combat the common danger. Only a carefully organized and rehearsed plan can assure a fast and effective response to any situation that may arise. Calm deliberation in the planning stage is required.

Disasters may be divided into two categories: natural and man-made. Natural disasters are all domestic emergencies except those created as a result of civil disturbance. Planning to meet disaster should be a continuing activity. Preparedness is an active state of mind. An installation ready for attack is better prepared to cope with natural disaster. Likewise, preparation for the effects of natural disaster may be considered a major step toward protection and recovery from any other type of emergency which may occur.

All effective countermeasures to disaster require some degree of prior planning: effectiveness is usually proportionate to the thoroughness and soundness of the planning effort, and there are underlying planning principles which, if followed, tend to produce sound plans, and which, if ignored, tend to produce unrealistic, unworkable plans. These principles apply to all aspects of survival planning—individual, family, community, or nation. Disaster need not mean catastrophe. Sound planning makes the difference.

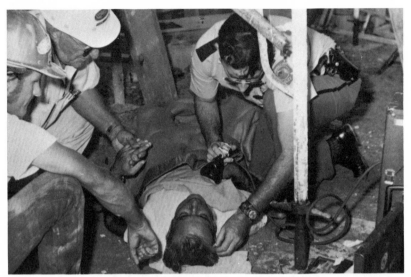

Figure 12. Emergencies arise when they are least expected. Security personnel must be prepared to deal with emergency situations immediately. All members of the security force should be thoroughly practiced in administering basic first-aid.

To be sound and realistic, disaster planning for any installation should adhere to the following concepts:

1. *Vulnerability Assessment.* A sound plan is based on a complete estimate of the situation; that is, a determination of the categories of disaster and the damage-causing factors to which the installation may be exposed. Internal vulnerability arises from the situation of, and conditions within, the installation itself. For instance, the site of an installation may make it particularly vulnerable to enemy attack or sabotage. External vulnerability is determined by the area in which the installation is located: geographical location in a hurricane belt makes an installation vulnerable to wind storm.

2. *Determination and Exploitation of Existing Capabilities.* A sound disaster emergency plan utilizes to the maximum the existing operational structure, proven supervisory and technical skills, and materiel on hand. Maximum effectiveness of emergency operations is attained when the unknown and variable factors in the situation are reduced to a minimum through prior planning. The disaster organization should be an extension of, not a substitute for, the organization which has proven effective in routine operations. Personnel who give directions in an emergency should be those from whom others are accustomed to receiving directions. The skill to perform specialized emergency tasks should be derived from

occupational and avocational background and interests. Emergency equipment should augment or supplement equipment on hand.

3. *Operational Readiness*. Plans alone will not guarantee survival, but sound plans in a state of operational readiness will increase the probability of survival. Operational readiness implies preparing the plan, training personnel in emergency responsibilities, testing the plans, evaluating the test, revising the plan as necessary, and constant retesting of the plan to insure its adequacy and workability in the event of disaster. Readiness cannot be accomplished if personnel are not familiar with the contents of the plan and their accorded responsibilities: information must be disseminated as needed to the individual employee, preferably by his supervisor.

Phases of Disaster Planning

The planning effort must be deliberate, systematic, and continuous if it is to be effective. This is achieved by phased planning with definite goals and targets for achievement of operational readiness.

Phase 1—Estimate of the Situation. Based upon the results of the vulnerability assessment, reduction of vulnerability where applicable, and resources available, an estimate is made to provide data for preparation of the plan.

Phase 2—Development of the Plan. This phase is the application of the principles of disaster planning to specific situations and the installation mission. It includes collecting resources, assigning and training personnel, and the preparation, coordination, and publication of planning documents.

Phase 3—Testing, Evaluation, and Revision. Upon completion of the disaster plan, provisions must be made for its testing and implementation. This is the phase in which deficiencies and unrealistic features are corrected. It validates the efforts previously made in preparation, training of personnel, and publishing the plan.

Disaster Plan Testing

It is essential that the following points be considered in testing the disaster plan:

1. Purpose of the test
   —To familiarize personnel with the contents of the plan.
   —To acquaint personnel with their emergency duties and responsibilities.
   —To evaluate the plan and determine its workability.
   —To identify deficiencies and make necessary corrections or adjustments.

2. Modes of testing the plan
   —Testing individual portions of the plan.
   —Testing one portion of the plan in conjunction with others.
   —Testing the complete disaster plan.
3. Conditions under which plans are tested to approximate realism
   —Simulated sabotage.
   —Simulated natural disaster.

Realism may be achieved by preparing appropriate situations and limiting knowledge of the type of situation to those preparing it.

Following are the methods of disseminating the information concerning the disaster plan.

1. Key personnel and supervisors should be briefed and should understand the plan as it affects them and their areas of responsibility. Each should have a copy of the plan.

2. Supervisors should have the responsibility of briefing personnel under their supervision. This briefing should be limited to an understanding of the plan in general, and details of the individual employee's responsibilities in implementing the disaster plan.

3. Notices on bulletin boards should be limited to action-type information. Posting of complete plans on bulletin boards is inadequate, as there is no guarantee that all personnel will read and understand the contents.

4. Utilization of an objective observer during the testing of a plan is suggested in order to have as complete and unbiased an opinion as possible. It is often difficult for one who has written a plan to detect any deficiencies which may exist. Special emphasis should be placed on observing actions of personnel and their state of training.

5. Deficiencies of unworkable procedures should be noted and indicated in the test critique. Other deficiencies that may endanger life or property should be corrected on the spot. After all deficiencies and unworkable parts of the plan have been noted and the plan reviewed, subsequent tests should be conducted to determine the validity of the plan.

6. No definite frequency can be established for tests. The plan should be tested initially in parts and then in its entirety. Further tests should be made as needed to keep personnel practiced on the provisions of the plan.

Emergency Control and Communications

The acid test of the disaster plan is a disaster situation calling for its implementation. How well the plan will work depends considerably upon preplanned control measures and previously arranged communications means. It follows that those responsible for disaster operations should be those responsible for disaster planning. In addition to the disaster control organization, the broad subject of control and communication is concerned with disaster control centers, internal and external communications, and warning systems.

In an emergency situation the ability to control is a function of the ability to communicate. The effective operation of the disaster control center will depend primarily upon the continuous functioning of its internal and external communications systems. In planning for communications, it must be considered that normal communications may break down in an emergency situation. Alternate means of communication must be provided.

An internal communications system capable of reaching the maximum number of the installation personnel is the desired goal for the installation. The emergency system should be built around and supplement the normal telephone intercom, public address, call bell, security force radio, and other radio systems in daily use. A realistic emergency repair and restoration plan for these systems must be established. Augmentation of existing systems should be made where possible by the addition of battery-powered, pack or hand-carried radio receiver-transmitter sets, and a battery or sound-powered, telephone system. These should be supplemented with a well-organized messenger service, and provisions should be made for regular inspection, maintenance, and testing of all systems.

Communications within the control center are simplified by centralizing all activity in one room. Personal contact, conference, and messenger service will satisfy the requirements in most centers. In very large operations a public address system may be utilized.

Warning Systems

An essential feature of any mechanical warning system is prompt and reliable operation. Careful planning, proper installation, and regular maintenance are necessary to insure that alarm sounding will start within a fraction of a minute after the warning signal has been received.

The disaster plan should make provision for notification of key personnel, including security force personnel, of any emergency situation which may develop during nonoperational hours. Initial notification of specific key personnel may be made the responsibility of the security force on duty. Each person called may be held responsible for notifying certain others.

Physical Security Plan—Outline and Format

I. *Purpose.* State purpose of the plan.

II. *Area Security.* Define the areas, buildings, and other structures considered critical and establish priorities for their protection.

III. *Control Measures.* Define and establish restrictions on access and movement into critical areas. These restrictions can be categorized as to personnel, vehicles, and materials.

    A. Personnel access

        1. Establish controls pertinent to each area or structure

           (i) Authority for access

           (ii) Access criteria for

                —Unit personnel

                —Visitors

                —Maintenance personnel

                —Contractor personnel

        2. Identification and control

           (i) Describe the system to be used in each area. If a badge system is used, a complete description covering all aspects should be used in disseminating requirements for identification and control of personnel conducting business on the installation.

    B. Application of the System

        1. Personnel

        2. Visitors to restricted areas

        3. Visitors to administrative areas

        4. Vendors, tradesmen, etc.

        5. Contractor personnel

        6. Maintenance or support personnel

    C. Materiel control

        1. Incoming

           (i) Requirements for admission of material and supplies

           (ii) Search and inspection of material for possible sabotage hazards

           (iii) Special controls on delivery of supplies and/or personnel shipments in restricted areas

        2. Outgoing

           (i) Documentation required

           (ii) Controls, as outlined in 1., (i), (ii), and (iii) above

           (iii) Classified shipments NOT involving nuclear material

   D. Vehicle control
      1. Policy on search of privately-owned vehicles
      2. Parking regulations
      3. Controls for entrance into restricted and administrative areas
         (i) Privately-owned vehicles
         (ii) Emergency vehicles
   E. Vehicle registration

IV. *Aids to Security*. Indicate the manner in which the following listed aids to security will be implemented on the installation.
   A. Perimeter barriers
      1. Definition
      2. Clear zones
         (i) Criteria
         (ii) Maintenance
      3. Signs
         (i) Types
         (ii) Posting
      4. Gates
         (i) Hours of operation
         (ii) Security requirements
         (iii) Lock security
      5. Maintenance and inspection
   B. Protective lighting system
      1. Use and control
      2. Inspection
      3. Action to be taken in the event of commercial power failure
      4. Action to be taken in the event of a failure of alternate source of power.
      5. Emergency lighting systems
         (i) Stationary
         (ii) Portable
   C. Alarm systems
      1. Security classification
      2. Inspection
      3. Use and monitoring
      4. Action to be taken in event of "Alarm" conditions
      5. Maintenance
      6. Alarm logs or registers
      7. Sensitivity settings
      8. Fail-safe and tamper-proof provisions

D. Communications
   1. Locations
   2. Use
   3. Tests
   4. Authentication

V. *Security Forces*. Include general instructions which would apply to all security force personnel. Detailed instructions such as Special Orders and SOP should be attached as annexes.

A. Composition and organization
B. Tour of duty
C. Essential posts
D. Weapons and equipment
E. Training
F. Use of sentry dogs
G. Method of challenging with sign and countersign
H. Alert force
   1. Composition
   2. Mission
   3. Weapons and equipment
   4. Location
   5. Deployment

VI. *Emergency Actions*. Indicate emergency actions of general application. Detailed plans such as disaster, fire, etc., should be attached as annexes.

A. Individual actions
B. Alert force
C. Security force actions

8

Pilferage

This chapter is designed to advise and guide physical security officers, police personnel, and specifically assigned Department of Defense civilian security police or guards in methods for controlling pilferage from consumer outlets and their storage facilities. Additionally, it is intended to provide guidance in evaluating physical security to officers-in-charge and managers (hereafter referred to as facility manager) of outlets which functionally have customer sales or service, transit, and supporting storage facilities. Included is information concerning conditions conducive to employee and patron pilferage; methods frequently used by employees and patrons; and enforcement and legal considerations associated with pilferers, pilferage, and its control.

Pilferage involves the deliberate attempt to circumvent human controls and physical security measures for personal gain. It is often the cause of the most costly and most frequent losses noted in consumer outlets and their associated storage facilities. Pilferage from consumer outlets and their storage facilities can be reduced and controlled through implementation of a well planned, comprehensive security plan.

Responsibilities

The manager is accountable or responsible for funds, subsistence, supplies or other property, employed or assigned personnel, and he controls all matters connected with the maintenance and operation of the facility under his charge. To accomplish this, he must at all times maintain adequate loss-prevention safeguards in the operation of the consumer outlet and associated storage facilities. Prevention of pilferage, and dismissal or other proper disposition of employees and patrons who actually engage in pilferage, is essential to proper operation of the total facility. It is incumbent upon the manager to work closely with the installation security off and those investigative or security personnel designated to support installation facilities in this manner.

Definitions

Storage Facilities. Those supply points, warehouses, holding areas and other functions which primarily receive and store stock for subsequent supply to consumer outlets.

Total Facility. The combination of total consumer outlets, related storage facilities and, where applicable, transit facilities connecting the foregoing as a part of the total sales, storage, supply complex.

The words *pilfer, pilferage,* and *shoplifting* are included within the meaning of steal, theft, larceny and other such terms implying theft of any quantity of any item of any monetary value.

Systematic Pilferer or Pilferage. An individual or system of stealing according to a preconceived plan or method with a motive for some form of personal profit. Frequently, but not necessarily, systematic pilfering is performed by more than one person. The pilferer may be an employee or patron of the facility.

Casual or Impulsive Pilferer. One who steals primarily because of impulse, temptation, need or an unexpected opportunity. He normally acts alone and may be an employee or patron of the facility. His pilferage is not planned or premeditated.

Diversionary Pilferage. Theft of facility commodities or stocks by diversion while they are in transit to the consumer outlet, warehouse or other proper destination. This is often accomplished by collusion between any combination of patrol, employee or other individuals. Diversion occurs at consumer outlets, warehouses, port facilities, loading docks, in transit or elsewhere in the supply line channel. Diversionary pilferage always involves systematic or prior planning.

Consumption Pilferage. The eating or using up of commodities or stock in the total facility. Usually this type of pilferage involves food, beverage or tobacco items. It may also include a broad range of non-consumables, such as personal or usable items that are figuratively consumed within the facility. Consumption pilferage may often account for a significant portion of the total pilferage loss.

Employee Pilferage

Employee pilferage generally involves, but is not limited to, systematic or diversionary pilferage from stocks located in either the consumer outlet, storage facilities, or in transit. This type of pilferage represents the largest potential loss.

Enforcement personnel may be assigned to investigate this type of pilferage or to make recommendations to reduce or control such activity. It is important that experienced personnel be used to investigate reported acts of pilferage and develop sound and effective recommendations for its control, based on (and in consonance with) the application of comprehensive physical security planning and measures for the entire facility.

Methods of Pilferage

Employee pilferage methods are often determined by the type and arrangement of existing physical facilities, routine operational procedures in use at consumer outlets or storage facilities, and the degree of assumed responsibility and alertness on the part of all assigned or employed personnel. Enforcement personnel must also be aware that the methods of employee pilferers may range from simple to complex systems, limited only by opportunity and the ingenuity of the individual pilferer. Following are some of the methods that have frequently been used and have accounted for substantial losses in consumer outlets.

1. Removal of shelf items, replacement stock, and other supplies when the consumer outlet is closed to patrons. Such pilferage often occurs at night or at other times when the merchandise is being restocked. Stolen property may be taken directly to personal vehicles or hidden in other predetermined locations. Employees may also hide property in empty cartons, garbage cans, or other refuse containers for subsequent removal from the consumer outlet, either with or without the knowledge and assistance of other employees. Such pilferage may include both perishable and nonperishable items.

2. Shelf items or merchandise normally kept in closed display cases, usually small in size and frequently of considerable relative value, may be hidden directly on the employee's person, in clothing or pocketbooks. Items may be added to shopping bags containing purchases employees have previously made. They may be pilfered from areas in the consumer outlet to which employees are not assigned or accountable but have uncontrolled access. Failure to inspect employee purchases and permitting employees to purchase at non-scheduled times and from other than designated personnel contributes to this method of pilferage.

3. Consumption pilferage, either systematic or casual, is frequently an overlooked or disregarded method of theft. Tobacco, edibles, beverages, clothing, cosmetics, and other personal items, to name only a few, are considered by some employees to be "fringe benefits" and are surreptitiously stolen and used in all areas of the total facility. Employees often retain these items, or the unused portions, for future use and keep them on their person, in pocketbooks, on shelves, under counters or at various other work areas in the consumer outlet or storage facilities.

4. Collusion may exist between vendor(s) and employee(s) of the consumer outlet, wherein the employee signs for more merchandise than was actually delivered. A cash or merchandise remuneration is then

obtained by the employee. This method is made particularly attractive to the dishonest employee when the commercial supplier personally fills consumer outlets' shelves or stores merchandise for subsequent employee-shelf stocking. The employee can remain remote from the vendor, the merchandise, and the mechanics of storage or stocking, and thereby appear uninvolved in this type of operation.

5. A comparable method of pilferage and remuneration exists in the collusion between employees and garbage or trash disposal personnel. In this system, packaged meats and other food items or stocks are picked up in a garbage or trash container and are later removed, used, or sold for profit.

Financial or other gain may be obtained by employees or patrons through the employee practice of providing unauthorized privileges or assisting in pilferage.

1. Employees may indirectly engage in theft by marking down valid merchandise prices for favored patrons or other employees. Reduced prices may be stamped directly on items, price tags may be altered or switched, or some other means can be used which simulates an authorized price reduction.

2. Employees may fraudulently declare merchandise old, shopworn, damaged or in the salvage category to cause price reduction. Numerous schemes are used, including false reporting of commodity condition, breaking or bending merchandise or containers, cutting seams on clothing and deliberately smudging or otherwise changing the external appearance of merchandise without materially altering its usefulness.

3. Theft also occurs indirectly through employees favoring their friends with extra amounts of merchandise, including foods and beverages served. Deliberately careless waste of foods and other perishable merchandise, or waste of expendable supplies used within the total facility, amounts to a substantial loss on an annual basis.

Numerous methods of pilferage, or combinations thereof, exist in the use of the cash register at patrol checkout and loading areas. Those that have a frequent and high loss-potential are listed below.

1. Direct theft of cash from register by the cashier or other employees.

2. Employees with after-hours access to the consumer outlet, or while unobserved, may rerun register tapes at lower figures, clear the register at the lowered total figure as actual receipts for the day, and pilfer the difference. Daily comparison by the facility manager or his representative of cash register lock and unlock numbers with previous operating day's numbers to insure continuous sequence will aid in detection of this type of pilferage.

3. Employees may pilfer items by obtaining a register tape from a prior valid patron purchase. This tape is attached to their own bag or package containing stolen property. Such bags may be placed in an open condition in waste baskets and used during the day as receptacles for both waste and pilfered items. At the end of the day they are stapled shut, with register tape attached, and carried out as a simulated valid purchase. For those employees who are authorized to purchase in the consumer outlet, the facility manager should daily designate one specific cash register through which the purchase will be recorded. The purchases will be made at the time the employee departs from work and the cash register tape will be marked by some means to preclude being reused. In addition, the purchases will be removed directly from the facility and not carried back through the sales area to another door for the employee's convenience.

4. By false reporting of overrings, cashiers may receive credit for the amount of alleged overringings and pilfer that amount of cash receipts.

5. Reporting of refunds for fictitious merchandise alleged to have been returned to consumer outlet stocks is another employee method of pilferage. The employee may then steal that amount of refund alleged to have paid out, first having falsified whatever required documentation and signatures are normally required on valid refunds to patrons.

6. A comparable method of pilferage may occur through collusion between an employee and a patron. In this method the patron signs falsified documentation alleging return of merchandise, required form(s) being provided by the employee, a refund is received and the patron and the employee benefit.

7. Deliberately underringing the cash register, through collusion between employee and patron, whereby amounts less than actual prices are rung up and the employee and/or the patron benefit.

8. Removal of items from bags or containers by bagboys and other carry-out employees may occur following valid patron payment. This may happen between the time the patron departs the checkout area and the time he returns with his vehicle. Both cashiers and bagboys may be involved, individually or in collusion.

Employee pilferage methods in storage facilities are also varied, limited only by opportunity, existing operational controls, and any physical security measures in effect. Some of the methods used include:

1. Removal of stock by unauthorized employees gaining access to service entrance keys or through unauthorized duplicate keys.

2. Removal of stock while storage facility doors are carelessly left open, or while doors, windows, and other openings are deliberately left unlocked. Employees also may intentionally hide or arrange to be locked inside the facility at the end of the work day (the so-called "stay behind"), thereby affording pilferage opportunity. Security personnel should check carefully

for such persons. All warehouse doors should be secured by padlocks and not just pins or bars for those doors normally secured from the inside, thus hindering, if not preventing, the "stay behind's" departure with pilfered items.

3. Deliberately careless or inaccurate accounting procedures when issuing or receiving storage facility stocks, thereby creating a surplus of stocks for which the employee is not accountable, and which he may later remove for his own use.

4. Removal of items from cartons or other containers, resealing the empty or partially empty containers, and returning them to storage or other proper location.

5. Alteration of stock records to cover up shortages of items previously stolen or intended for future pilferage. Merchandise or stocks scheduled for such systematic pilferage may already be in the storage facility, en route, or pending delivery. Carriers as well as warehouse or storage facility personnel may be in collusion in this type of activity. Stock scheduled for pilferage may include clothing, food, automotive items, hardware, electrical appliances, or any similar items often in the high-value, low-bulk category.

6. Removal from carriers of in-transit merchandise at unscheduled stops or at unprotected departure and arrival points. Such diversionary pilferage almost always requires collusion between employees of the facility and delivery or carrier personnel. Organizational structure and equipment for pilferage operations may be very extensive, including personnel, vehicles, and entire facilities.

7. Deliberate falsification of internal inventories, issue and receipt records, and other accountability documentation when inventories and/or audits are conducted by other than honest, qualified, or disinterested personnel.

Conditions Conducive to Employee Pilferage

There are numerous factors which contribute or are conducive to employee pilferage. These generally fall into two basic categories: inadequate physical security measures and inadequate or insufficient utilization of human resources in the areas of management, training, discipline, responsibility, and other control measures. Of the two categories, human resource factors are more subject to breakdown, fluctuation, inadequacy, and neglect.

At the management or top supervisory level, the failure to have or implement a proper plan or organization, the lack of adequate methods and measures to safeguard assets, checks to control and insure accuracy and reliability of accounting procedures, stress in the promotion of operational efficiency, and encouragement to comply with prescribed policies all contribute to employee pilferage in the total facility. Some of the negative factors conducive to employee pilferage are:

1. Failure to set the best example by continuing interest, motivation, direction and alertness to internal control of pilferage.

2. Failure to delegate responsibility clearly, to insist upon and stress the requirement for responsible accountability, and to properly train and orient, with clear, firm guidelines, other supervisors in the operation of their departments.

3. Inadequate or nonexistent written rules of conduct, standards of job performance, and orientation of new and current employees, including penalties for theft and other infractions (discharge, and possible prosecution).

Midgrade supervisors and other employees also contribute to pilferage in consumer outlets and storage facilities by the foregoing acts of omission or inadequacy. Other deficiencies at this level may include:

1. Inadequate or infrequent inspection and monitoring of all facility operations at regular and unannounced intervals, to include checking formal accounting and inventory records for accuracy and completeness.

2. Permitting employees with custody or access to merchandise or stocks to have unmonitored access to (and the opportunity to alter) official stock records.

3. Careless and disorganized storage or stocking of consumer outlet merchandise, which makes accurate and rapid inventory difficult, contributing to and encouraging surreptitious pilferage of various types.

4. Permitting unscheduled rest periods, leaving assigned work areas unprotected and granting unlimited access to other facility areas.

5. Failure to notify appropriate consumer outlet or enforcement personnel when employees are known to have been stealing or when there is valid reason to believe pilferage has occurred. Included is failure to cooperate fully by providing information and suggestions when crime prevention or physical security inspections or surveys are being conducted, or when enforcement personnel are investigating pilferage of property or funds.

Other conditions conducive to employee pilferage relate to inadequate or nonexistent physical security measures and/or human failure in application of those that do exist. Physical security officers must recommend and follow up on corrective measures. Some typical areas where physical security may be nonexistent or deficient include:

1. Exterior lighting in vehicle parking areas, building perimeters, including fences, doors, windows, loading docks and ramps and other critical areas.

2. Interior lighting of security storage areas or bins, cashier cages, safes and registers and other departmental areas where critical stock or merchandise is stored or displayed on shelves, in cases, or other locations.

3. Barriers, including fences, gates, and doors, screening or bars on windows, vents and crawl spaces, and warning and/or other cautionary signs and instructional media posted on such barriers.

4. Vehicle control of privately-owned vehicles by requiring parking in designated areas away from entrance and service doors, loading areas and employees.

5. Intrusion-detection alarm systems on exterior and/or interior areas, buildings, security rooms for highly pilferable expensive items, and other locations of criticality of property or vulnerability to unauthorized entry.

6. Lock security and control.

7. Structural characteristics of building, doors and windows, security storage areas and cages.

8. Placement, location and dimensions of shelves, display cases, counters, aisles, shopping islands and other comparable areas within the consumer outlet.

Techniques for Detecting Pilferage

Techniques for detecting pilferage vary somewhat, dependent upon the type, location and size of the consumer outlet and storage facilities. Primarily, techniques are based upon observation of employee conduct, physical evidence indicative of pilferage, internal controls established by the consumer outlet officer or supervisor(s), physical aids or adjuncts in use, and appropriate investigative measures employed by enforcement personnel.

The pilferer may be observed in his theft by actual consumption of goods or by an overt act of pilferage. More often his behavior, appearance, job performance, selection of and conduct with associates, and compliance or noncompliance with existing rules or policies will be indicative of preparation for, or acts of, covert pilferage. Work habits, traits or mannerisms, clothing, and other indicators not consistent with normal efficient work production should be observed and evaluated carefully.

In consumer outlets, physical evidence of pilferage may be indicated by the unusual movement, disruption, and placement of warehouse stocks or displayed items. Empty of partially empty cartons, broken cases, cut, torn or refastened container flaps, and variations in weight of like items should all be considered. Particular attention should be given to locations such as rest areas and employee lounges, employee parking areas, isolated corners or sections of storage areas, garbage trash containers and removal locations, rest rooms and any other locations where employees may gather, loiter or find temporary privacy.

Frequent excuses, disappearances, or unscheduled absences of employees may be indicative of pilferage. Those employees who work with minimal supervision and leave their normal work areas for questionable reasons or who are observed in locations not consistent with their duties warrant particular attention. Day-to-day conversations, either heard or reported, should be evaluated for signs of collusion between employees, vendors, and patrons.

Current and well-kept records may indicate abnormal losses or shortages of stocks if not reconciled by inventory or rebalance of accounts, and may provide important investigative information. Shelves and displays that appear to be unusually empty or seem to indicate that items are rapid sellers should be viewed with suspicion when not verified by actual records of estimated sales volume. Cashier tapes and other records which reveal shortages, overages of other imbalance on a consistent basis may indicate that money is being pilfered from cash receipts, working funds, bank deposits and other sources. Careful scrutiny should be directed to changes, alterations and remade records, tapes, deposit slips, ledgers and other means of recording funds and property.

Surprise cash counts, spot checks of storage areas, refrigeration units, displays, shelves, fitting rooms, garment racks, employee purchases, and other informal inventory measures should be conducted frequently but at irregular and unannounced times.

Information may be developed from employees or other personnel who have knowledge of pilferage. The degree of loss from pilferage may justify the use of paid informers, but because their motives vary, such information must be carefully evaluated. Employees are in a good position to detect irregularities and should be encouraged to report such activities through a sense of duty and responsibility.

Physical security inspections disclose areas of weakness in the total facility, providing information indicative of pilferage. Subsequent investigation, and interviews of personnel or interrogations of suspects and apprehended pilferers may lead to the identification of other pilferage activities and suspects.

Other indications of pilferage may be obtained from the results of screening personnel records, reports from local law enforcement agencies, anonymous tips, undercover enforcement personnel, and other sources which can be effectively used to detect pilferage or provide information concerning potential pilferage targets. There is no substitute for ingenuity, alertness and continuing vigilance on the part of those concerned with pilferage detection and prevention.

Methods of Controlling Pilferage

The basic *control* methods are the correction of conditions *conducive* to pilferage and the use of proven techniques to detect them. All logical, economically feasible measures should be taken to correct those physical and human resource deficiencies which were enumerated. In the design and layout of new or renovated facilities, physical security measures should be included to amplify the control of pilferage activities. Following are some of the basic considerations for all facilities, including physical security and internal control measures.

Sufficient lighting on fences, shipping and receiving areas, and building exteriors, including doors, windows, and other possible points of entrance, will increase protective night time security. Fixed-position lights should be of a diffused type to minimize shadows. Security lighting should be used at night in any room or area containing funds or critical (high-cost, easily pilferable) supplies. Safes should be visible to guards, police or other enforcement personnel.

Security of combination number lists, keys, facility locks and allied containers is of major importance. Keys and lists of combinations should be secured in an approved container with limited access to this repository. A minimum number of keys—an issue consistent with operational necessity—should be available. Key and combination issues should be recorded, with regular turn-in and inventory accountability maintained. Combinations, padlocks, or lock cylinders should be changed whenever employees with access to them rotate or terminate employment. Because keys and combinations may be compromised, duplicated, lost or obtained by unauthorized personnel, combinations, locks or lock cylinders should be changed every 12 months, or more frequently if circumstances require. All safes, cabinets and locking devices should comply with current federal specifications. Padlocks should be snapped shut on locking staples or hasps of opened doors or containers. This will preclude the surreptitious substitution, with a comparable lock having a key(s) or known combination, for the lock currently in use. Seals, with numbers recorded, may be placed on various types of critical storage areas or containers to disclose damage or tampering.

Where warranted, fences, gates and other barriers should be constructed for perimeter security and to channel vehicle and pedestrian movement. Consideration should be given to placing bars or security screening on all external doors, windows, and other possible points of entrance. Construction of window and door frames, supports and framing for internal security rooms, cages and other critical areas, should be substantial, preferably of masonry or metal, to increase security of attached bars or security screening.

Design and layout of storage and shopping areas should consider limiting the height of stocks and displays and the placement or number of cross aisles to preclude blind spots and poorly lighted secluded areas.

Parking of privately-owned vehicles should be rigidly controlled, as previously stated. The use of privately-owned vehicles for the transportation of facility stocks or supplies and funds should be prohibited, and unannounced searches of transporting vehicles should be scheduled at irregular intervals. Semi-trailers and other vehicles with detached or separated driver and load compartments may be locked and sealed, with seal numbers recorded, at the point of departure. Upon arrival, seals should be inspected for tampering and proper number, and the load compartment should be unlocked by authorized receiving personnel. With this system the driver does not have keys to his cargo and is partially relieved of responsibility, temptation, and threats to cargo pilferage. Empty carriers or containers may be locked or sealed to deter pickup of pilfered items after unloading or in transit.

Consideration should be given to the use of guards around or within potentially vulnerable areas. A critical evaluation should be made to assess the effective use and placement of existing or contemplated protective personnel. The security posture of facilities may be additionally strengthened by installation of intrusion-detection devices or alarm systems on buildings, rooms, safes, containers and other critical areas or locations. Notification of intrusion or alarm should be received at locations where rapid response is possible. Such systems may be of significant aid in timely response to attempted pilferage and apprehension of persons responsible.

Internal Controls

The following may be used as a general checklist on internal controls to prevent pilferage; other items may be added as necessary or desirable in the individual situation.

Control Over Receiving Operations
1. Maintenance of receiving logs
2. Short-shipment, overage and damage reports
3. Bulk checking
4. Receiving directly on sales floor

Proper Marking of Merchandise
1. Authorized source of prices
2. Selection of proper type tickets
3. Checking accuracy of tickets
4. Method of printing prices to prevent changing
5. Use of "hidden" tickets
6. Bulk marking

Proper Remarking and Price Changing
1. Authorized source of prices
2. Methods of reticketing

3. Methods of price changing
4. Special sales
5. Customer allowances
6. Control over price change documents

Invoice Payment
1. Authorization for payment
2. Prevent duplicate payment

Maintenance of Accurate Book Inventory
1. Document control
2. Checking purchase records
3. Rechecking arithmetic

Sales Floor Control
1. Protection of high value merchandise
2. Prohibit employees from "holding" merchandise
3. Prohibit employees from "borrowing" merchandise
4. Internal register control
5. Blind spot (eliminate)
6. Floor coverage by responsible personnel
7. Fitting room control
8. Consumption or use of inventory
9. Measuring and weighing
10. Price discrepancies
11. Unmarked merchandise

Cash Register Areas
1. Keep clear of merchandise
2. Overring or error control
3. Cash pickups
4. Cash drawer responsibility
5. Cashier-packer combinations
6. Pricing unmarked merchandise
7. Checking-out relatives
8. Checking-out employees
9. Stubbing of tickets
10. Control over stubs
11. Proper ringing of department keys
12. Proper ringing of taxes
13. Getting change during day
14. Recognition of counterfeit bills
15. Sealing of packages
16. Ticket stapling
17. Check cashing
18. Examination of shopping baskets and bags

Refund and Exchange Controls
1. Controlled issuance of refund voucher pads
2. Authorization of refunds
3. Compare refunded merchandise with refund vouchers
4. Charging proper concessions with refunds
5. Security of refund pads
6. Letters to customers, checking refunds
7. Control over exchanges

Layaway Control
1. Use of layaway registers
2. Control over layaway cards
3. Daily summary of layaway transactions
4. Security of layaway merchandise
5. Limit employee layaways
6. Comparing layaway merchandise and cards
7. Frequent layaway clearance
8. Reconciliation of running balance due with layaway cards, balance due with layaway cards, balance total

Employee Purchase Control
1. Authorization and inspection
2. Sealing of packages
3. Recording of purchases
4. Predesignating register

Control of Employee Packages, Garments and Handbags
1. Employee outer garments in secure area
2. Employee handbag control
3. Employee package control

Returns to Vendors
1. Control over charge-back forms
2. Control over charge-back and quantity
3. Control over shipment to vendor

Inter-Store Transfers
1. Control over documents
2. Control over price and quantity transferred

Disposition of Damaged Merchandise
1. Prohibit immediate price reductions by clerks for customers

2. Define authority to change price
3. Return of damaged goods to vendors
4. Prohibit employee purchases of damaged merchandise
5. Define method of disposing of unsalable goods

Physical Security
1. Doors
2. Windows
3. Alarms
4. Safe
5. Registers
6. Cashier's office
7. Stockrooms
8. Receiving doors
9. Trash pickup
10. Truck depots
11. Key control
12. Night lockup
13. Employee parking
14. Cleaning crews

Security Policies
1. Prosecution of dishonest employees
2. Fraternization of employees with patrons
3. Prosecution of shoplifters
4. Gambling by employees
5. Employment of relatives

Shoplifting Prevention
1. Employee training program
2. Employee reward program
3. Strict prosecution policy

Patron Pilferage

Patron pilferage (shoplifting) is usually confined to the sales areas of consumer outlets, since patrons have no general authorized access to storage areas and are subject to recognition and questioning when observed in such areas. Patron pilferers may be either casual or systematic pilferers; they may operate alone, with patron associates, or with employees of the consumer outlet.

The items most frequently pilfered by patrons in consumer outlets are relatively small in size and have a high degree of consumer desirability. They often are easily carried in shopping bags or pocketbooks or secreted on the person. The category range of articles is extensive and includes

Figure 13. Highly visible security personnel will often discourage shoplifters in retail outlets.

foods, clothing, household supplies and numerous other personally desirable or resalable articles. Effective security measures, proper training and use of employee personnel and adequate opertional guidance can effectively reduce patron pilferage.

Common Types of Shoplifters

The Amateur Adult Shoplifter:
1. Sudden temptation-impulse theft. Success in initial thefts results in more temptation, stronger impulses, more thefts.
2. Need. Sometimes (though rarely) the theft reflects a genuine need for the item, or the money it can be sold for. Generally, however, the shoplifter has enough money with him or her to pay for the items taken, and stealing was an "economy" measure.
3. Given time, however, amateurs become as skilled as professionals and must be handled with this danger in mind. The seriousness of the offense, and its legal consequences, must be made clear to the amateur if this course is to be interrupted.
clear to the amateur if this course is to be interrupted.

The Juvenile Shoplifter:
1. Takes small "luxury" items for own use.
2. May shoplift on a dare or to belong.

3. May work in gangs, distracting customers and salespeople by noisy, disorderly behavior, covering for the actual theft.

4. Some juveniles are coached and directed by an adult, who may have accompanied them to the store. Every effort should be made to identify and apprehend these adults.

The Professional Shoplifter:

1. May be talkative, is usually polite and deliberate.

2. Makes a career of it, often undergoing systematic training. Takes pride in his or her skill and has no desire to reform. Often works in association with other professionals sometimes traveling throughout the country.

3. Does not take many chances. Will desist if time is not opportune and will "dump" merchandise, often openly, if spotted.

4. Is shrewd in spotting a detective.

5. Likes to take valuable, salable merchandise, often $300 a day or more, but prefers a three-day work week. Steals in quantity.

6. Steals for resale; usually has "fences" or contacts, sometimes a bargain shop where items are resold. Often "steals to order" and may have a list of sizes and colors. Often sells to "respectable" citizens, who deny any knowledge that goods bought at 25% of store cost were stolen.

7. Will use shoplifting "appliances," such as the "booster box," coat-length pockets, hooks on belt, etc.

8. May have a long record of arrests, is difficult to convict, and often manages to get off with a light sentence. (Pessimistic as this latter point may sound, most experienced retail people recommend that professionals be prosecuted without exception; such a policy is reported to other professionals, deterring them from working that store.

The Kleptomaniac:

1. Takes items without regard to value or use.

2. Steals compulsively, often openly. Repeats, even after several apprehensions. May come from any station in life; may be a male or female.

3. Is a more definite type, nervous and shy, although a few are arrogant. (Genuine cases of kleptomania are rare. Compulsive theft, true kleptomania, is said to resemble the aberration of the "fire-bug," particularly as to the type of person and the gratification gained by the act. A similar theft problem to the kleptomaniac is the shoplifter, usually young, who steals openly and seems to "want to be caught." Usually a troubled youngster indirectly seeking help, these cases respond more readily to psychiatric treatment.)

The Shoplifter-Addict:

1. The narcotics addict turned shoplifter is the most dangerous to apprehend because of his desperate need for money and fear of imprison-

ment. Shoplifting and burglary are the two most common means used by addicts to get money for their habit.

2. The addict takes chances; does not stall but snatches merchandise and makes a quick getaway.

3. When an addict steals he is usually at his lowest ebb, and his unusual behavior may allow him to be identified.

4. Is dangerous to handle, will habitually resist apprehension, often violently. Addicts should be handled only by police officers, though a trained and experienced security officer can handle these cases. All agree, however, that other store personnel should *not* attempt to apprehend an addict. Local law officers are the best source of information on the frequency and the kinds of addicts which might be encountered locally, as well as what to watch for.

The Vagrant and The Alcoholic Shoplifter:

1. Is often under the influence of liquor at the time of the theft.

2. Usually is the "snatch and run" type.

3. May be "floater"; is less likely to repeat regularly at a single location.

4. If a vagrant, usually has a police record.

5. Vagrants and alcoholics are relatively easy to identify because of their appearance, and should be watched carefully when seen.

Methods of Patron Pilferage

Patrons' methods for pilfering are in a constant state of modification and improvement and involve varying degrees of ingenuity, often dependent upon the presence or absence and degree of alertness of employees. Pilferers are primarily concerned with obtaining and secreting items while in the consumer outlet, avoiding detection, circumventing payment at registers or checkout areas, and subsequently departing from the premises. Some of the various techniques used are as follows:

1. Loose-fitting clothing can be used to conceal a large quantity of pilfered items. Hidden pockets or false linings are sometimes sewn into garments. Tightly cuffed loose sleeves of coats and jackets may be used for concealment.

2. Pocketbooks and handbags are often carried on the forearm, in shopping carts, and in an opened condition, providing convenient places to drop pilfered items. The favorite place for women shoppers to hide items is in a purse; for men in their pockets. Also attractive to amateurs—and dangerous to the store—are shopping bags, bags or boxes from other stores, umbrellas, schoolbooks (for stealing records), knitting bags, and lunch boxes. Lipsticks and jewelry can be hidden in a soft drink purchased at a snack bar within the stores. Beware of the woman shopper who carries

her purse open under her arm with her change purse held prominently in her other hand. Her equivalent in supermarkets places the open purse on top in the grocery cart, handy for "accidentally" dropping in small, high-priced items.

3. Umbrellas caried in loose or partly opened positions are used to hide small items such as pens, jewelry or other lightweight and often elongated articles. Umbrellas may then be closed when approaching checkout areas. Boots, raincoats and other extra clothing worn during inclement weather also offer concealment.

4. Boxes or paper sacks which contain merchandise paid for at other departments may be opened and then reclosed after adding pilfered items. Accumulated, empty paper sacks may be filled with pilfered items and stapled with outdated cash register tapes from prior purchases. These then appear to be current, paid for, and are taken from the consumer outlet.

5. Folded magazines or newspapers, which are often hand-carried, may be used to hide small, flexible, pilfered items such as gloves, stockings and other clothing. Many other small articles in packages or bottles or other containers, are often hidden in folds of a rolled newspaper.

6. Hats, gloves, scarves, coats, sweaters and purses are often worn out of the store.

7. Coats or sweaters may be thrown down over merchandise desired, and picked up with the merchandise concealed inside.

8. Trying things on "for effect"—jewelry can be unclasped and allowed to drop within the neckline; sweaters or blouses tucked inside a suit jacket "to see how it looks" can be "forgotten" and worn out of the store. Patting or "arranging" the back of the hair can "cover" for dropping a small item down the neck of a dress.

9. The fitting room "shell game"—Tight or closely fitting garments can be put on under street clothes. Packages and purse can be arranged to conceal the addition of a dress or blouse. Methods for failure to return merchandise to the racks include such ruses as getting more than the permitted number of dresses without the knowledge of a clerk, and the returning only of the permitted number while she is busy with another customer. Two women in one dressing room, each with the allotted number, or with one going back and forth with garments for the other to "try on," can often confuse salespersons as to the number of garments taken, and the number returned to the racks. The "difficult to please, hard to fit" customer who sends the salesperson back many times for additional garments to try on also uses this ruse. Frequent clearing of dressing rooms to remove "surplus" garments is a necessity in guarding against this technique. Occasional surveillance of dressing rooms by female operators, with or without suspicion having been aroused, has also proved effective.

10. Handling several articles, as though for inspection, often reaching between customers, enables the shoplifter to ostentatiously return part of

the merchandise while secreting the remainder. A variation of this is getting the clerk to display more stock than he or she can keep track of.

11. Stepping around the end of counters "to see something." Expensive articles are often lifted from inside unlocked show cases.

12. A method rising in popularity involves "switching tickets" on merchandise; putting a ticket for a lesser amount on a garment in place of the garment's higher ticket. Another version "marks down" the label in a forgery of the store's method of hand-written repricing. It is for this reason that the repricing should be done off the floor and in a manner that discourages forgery. Ticket-switching is difficult to "pin" on the shoplifter, who denies any responsibility for the wrong ticket being on the merchandise. Some retail special agents are going to fingerprinting, to prove that the higher ticket (usually found replacing the lower tickets) bears the fingerprints of the shoplifter. This method is also common in supermarkets, where labels are switched or pasted over genuine price labels.

13. "Palming" is the simplest and most common method for removal of small articles. It is difficult to detect, even while watching. It consists of placing an open hand on a small article, squeezing the muscles of the hand over the article to grasp it, and lifting the still open and apparently empty hand. Palming is often aided by the use of a package, hankerchief, or gloves, etc., and an accomplice may stand to screen the shoplifter. Many shoplifters are as skilled at palming as a sleight-of-hand performer. Watch their hands; know your stock.

14. Children are sometimes trained to pilfer, articles desired being pointed out by the adult. If caught, the adult may apologize and "scold" the child for his theft. Adults may also hide pilfered items under clothing worn by small children who may be riding in shopping carts, or within toys that children may be carrying. Baby carriages, as well as any personal items deposited in them, are convenient locations to hide stolen articles.

15. Patron pilferers frequently convert stolen items into cash refunds. This often involves bringing to the consumer outlet a hidden empty bag and a cash register receipt from a former valid purchase. The pilferer then steals some of the same or same priced items formerly purchased, presents the bags, stolen items, receipt, and requests a refund. This is usually accompanied by an explanation that the items are not needed, do not fit, or are in some other way inadequate.

Other methods of patron pilferage exist, including pilferage by consumption and through acts of collusion with consumer outlet employees. A review of methods will disclose that with applicable modification, some employee methods may also be used by patrons. The confidence, dexterity, and ingenuity of accomplished shoplifters is formidable.

Conditions Conducive to Patron Pilferage

Many of the conditions conducive to employee pilferage are conducive to patron pilferage as well.

Patron pilferage, or shoplifting, is generally made possible or easier by untrained, inexperienced, or indifferent employees. Through lack of training, lack of interest in customers, or lack of supervision, they fail to observe the conduct of persons around them. Insufficient or inefficient employees also contribute to the general problem. Pilferage is greatest when employee coverage is low or absent.

A failure to evaluate and correct inefficient floor plans and layout contributes to pilferage potential. Patron traffic flow, small rooms or partitioned areas, congested conditions, narrow aisles and partially hidden or isolated displays are some of the factors to be considered.

Nonexistent or insufficient patron guidance and rules of shopping create unnecessary confusion, congestion, and operational problems. Adequate warning signs or printed instructions which are firmly enforced should outline required identification media, ages of patrons (if applicable), use of privately-owned shopping carts, admission of packages, baby strollers or other articles. Shopping carts should remain in the sales area, thereby precluding the possibility of items remaining on the lower shelf of the cart and not being recorded at the cash register.

Mechanical Devices Used in Shoplifting

Special shoplifting devices multiply the amount of merchandise that can be removed from the store in a single trip. Because they mark the shoplifter as a professional, they are avoided by those shoplifters hoping to pose as amateurs overcome by temptation.

Most famous of shoplifting devices is the "booster box," usually larger than a suit-box and tied with string. The box may be wrapped in brown paper, and even ostensibly addressed for mailing. Actually, one end of the box is free to fold in, and shoplifted garments are thrust through this opening. A variation of the booster box is a box or purse designed to be put down over the object desired. When the box is lifted, the object is "gone."

Various devices are used under coats, trousers, skirts and dresses. Belts with eyelets or hooks hold merchandise suspended around the waist under a coat. Special pockets can hold as much as a full bolt of cloth. Slits conceal extra pockets. "Booster bloomers" worn under full skirts permit dropping large quantities of small items into the waistband.

Use of Accomplices in Shoplifting

Any disturbance should prompt extra attention to every customer's actions. Ways in which accomplices facilitate shoplifting include:

1. Standing as a shield; acting as a lookout.

2. Engaging the attention of the salesperson while the "husband" or "wife" strolls about the department, coat over arm.

3. Moving high-value merchandise to another rack, easier to pick up from and more remote from salespersons.

4. Holding the pilfered merchandise. Transferring stolen items to a confederate is an old dodge that is still all too successful. It is the reason for the rule "If you lose sight of the shoplifter for an instant, never apprehend." The legal consequences of arrest without evidence of theft are too serious to be ignored.

5. Creating a disturbance. This can range from the man who accompanied his wife, pushing a stroller containing triplet babies, to noisy disturbances by gangs of teenagers. Besides shoplifting, disturbances are used to cloak thefts from cash registers.

6. The "unseen" confederate. The customer who attracts suspicion, and hence attention, or who takes a lot of waiting on, or who gets into an argument with the salesperson may be giving a confederate a chance to get away with valuable merchandise. Fainting and falling are other ruses that come in this category.

Techniques for Detecting and Controlling Pilferage

Patron pilferage can usually be detected by alert visual observation on the part of all employees. Such observation will disclose thefts as they occur, reveal conditions and mannerisms indicative of such pending or completed acts, and indicate physical evidence that concealment of stolen items is contemplated or has been accomplished.

Some indicators that systematic or casual pilferage may be intended, or may have occurred, are often the following:

1. Patrons may be observed wearing loose-fitting clothing, frequently not consistent with weather conditions or the locale.

2. Shopping carts or hand-carried baskets may contain partially open umbrellas, shopping bags, purses or loosely folded clothing, all of which are potential places of concealment. Shoulder bags or coats and jackets draped over an arm also offer hiding places.

3. Patrons who appear to be wandering aimlessly in the consumer outlet, particularly during slack periods, may be waiting for a shoplifting opportunity.

4. Repetitive and blasé actions may be indicative of pilferage in progress. These might include bending over to tie shoe laces, picking up items deliberately dropped, or opening and reclosing items of clothing being worn. All of these may indicate that items are being secreted somewhere on the person, or the pilferer, thinking he is being observed, is

attempting to affect a casual manner. Prolonged or minute examination of merchandise may also be suspect as a delaying tactic for pilferage opportunity.

5. Pilferers sometimes engage employees, more than one if possible, in conversations, requests for assistance, or questions not readily answered. Employees so tricked into providing service in one area permit a confederate shoplifter to pilfer more easily in another.

6. Juvenile pilferers often show the same traits as adults and employ comparable tactics. They may be more brazen in actions and chances taken, sometimes creating a nuisance or other diversionary situations while dispersed members of the group are stealing.

7. Detection is sometimes possible by observing the shopping habits of patrons. Pilferers desire brief periods of isolation and may be noted in vacant or near-empty aisles, at ends of display gondolas or near exits. They frequently move about the outlet in direct relationship to the proximity of employees. The accomplished shoplifter generally tries to appear casual, does not hurry or act impulsively, and attempts to match the mood, actions, and appearance of other shopping patrons. Close attention should be directed to composure, facial expressions and mannerisms, to observe signs betraying either their intent or their attempts to determine if others are watching them.

8. Employees should be friendly and helpful to patrons. Observation of patrons who appear to be unusually friendly, or who seem to be particularly eager to cultivate friendships with certain employees, may expose a pilferer.

9. Physical evidence may be indicative that patron pilferage has occurred. Empty cartons, small boxes or other containers may be found on shelves, in shopping carts, on floors or other locations. Such evidence should suggest the possibility that items have been consumed or hidden. It might also indicate attempts to reduce the possibility of identification of the item as being from outlet stocks, or to imply prior possession, through removal of original containers, price tags or other markings.

Methods of controlling patron pilferage vary and are primarily dependent upon existing conditions conducive to pilferage, the degree of pilferage, activity, and techniques employed by pilferers. Where applicable, the following controls will reduce pilferage and the vulnerability of the facility to such activity.

1. Shopping areas should be well lighted at all times. Display areas and aisles should provide adequate space to avoid congestion.

2. Displays should not be of a height that provides concealment for shoppers, standing upright, isolated areas, rooms and cross aisles which permit movement from "line of sight" should be reduced to a minimum.

3. The least number of doors, consistent with safety or fire regulations, should be operational. The entrance door(s) should be monitored, and only

authorized persons granted entry, to reduce pilferage opportunity. Required emergency exit doors, not under visual observation, may have warning devices installed to indicate when they are opened.

4. Consumer outlets should be neat and orderly at all times. Empty containers and other unremoved refuse, disorganized or carelessly stocked shelves or displays, and similar conditions of disorder indicate to the pilferer a general indifference to security or efficient facility operations.

5. Critical items, usually those of relatively high cost and small size which can be easily pilfered, should be placed near and in view of cashiers. Such items may also be displayed in locked cases or on back shelves where patron access is difficult and noticeable. The number of such items on display should be kept to a minimum and checked continually.

6. The use of wall or ceiling-hung mirrors, closed-circuit TV cameras (live and dummy), alarm or warning devices on safes, display cases, or other critical locations, posted warning signs to pilferers, and other physical security aids should be considered.

7. The facility manager should carefully consider and evaluate the assignment of trusted employee(s) to the additional (or separate) duty of being alert to and monitoring pilferage activities, related employee conduct, and compliance with anti-pilferage procedures and regulations. The need for, and duties of, such employee personnel will be determined by the size floor plan and complexity and the amount of pilferage detected at the facility.

8. Pilferage activity may indicate the need for assignment of enforcement personnel to undercover positions within the total facility. The existing situation will often determine the number, desired capabilities, and sex of such personnel.

Although conditions and requirements may be widely varied, such personnel should generally be emotionally mature, intelligent, alert and adaptive to changing requirements and situations under stress conditions.

The most effective and economical method of controlling patron pilferage is through the individual employee. Effective human control can never be adequately replaced by physical security devices or systems alone. Some of the initial controls applicable are:

1. Effective screening and selection of new employees, to include background data as to character and integrity, as well as current ability to perform adequately.

2. Realistic orientation given new employees in the area of job discipline, loyalty and responsibility, to include penalties for theft, collusion in stealing, and other violations.

3. Specific training or refresher orientation for all employees concerning effective methods and procedures to safeguard assets, operational methods that insure accuracy and reliability of accounting

procedures for monies and commodities, and the various sales controls and practices that aid in pilferage reduction. Included should be explanations stressing how and why such controls are important to the operation of the facility and the well-being of employees and employer.

Employees who have direct contact with patrons can most effectively curb and reduce patron pilferage by their observation and subsequent actions. Preventive measures require a conscientious alertness and awareness of persons, surroundings and situations during performance of duties. Some of the more common employee actions which assist in pilferage prevention and control include the following:

1. Employees should arrange displays so that items are easily seen and require minimal patron handling for adequate examination. Consideration should be given to limiting the number of like items on display at any one time, to permit easier observation and continuous visual inventory of stock.

2. Assigned employee areas should not be left vacant and unprotected. Employees temporarily less busy should observe surrounding areas to help cover for fellow workers. Employees working the entire floor should be alert, circulate, and watch for trouble areas or situations.

3. An effort should be made to remember faces. Shoplifters often return more frequently than other patrons, meanwhile buying less. Their suspected or known identity should be relayed to other concerned employees and enforcement personnel.

4. Service that is provided quickly and efficiently aids the valid patron relationship. Pilferers do not appreciate close attention and efficiency, but rather, employees who engage in needless conversation with each other or friends, or are "too busy" to help.

5. Items that are held by patrons while they show price markings and offer payment should be checked. Price tags may have been altered or switched, or container covers and caps exchanged, to indicate lower price markings.

6. When possible, merchandise being rung up on registers at checkout stations or at floor registers should be touched, lifted and examined by cashiers. Weight and feeling may indicate added items hidden within containers. When believed necessary, employees need not be hesistant about a careful item examination.

7. Sales, refunds, exchanges and other transactions should be recorded or accomplished promptly and only by authorized employees. Merchandise should be wrapped, tagged, stapled or otherwise identified properly in accordance with an effective policy that indicates payment has been made.

8. Suggestions from employees on methods to increase security should be encouraged and carefully evaluated. Effective ideas at the operational

level frequently elude supervisors or management due to remoteness from the problem.

9. Consumer outlets that present the appearance and atmosphere of courteous and alert efficiency enhance overall physical security. This condition can best be attained by well-supervised employees, properly trained and motivated, who are neat, courteous and efficient, and perform their duties and serve patrons to the best of their ability. Such attitudes and traits do much to reduce and control all types of pilferage, both patron and employee, and to increase operational effectiveness.

Suggestions for Store Management on Shoplifting

1. Determine what areas of the sales floor are most vulnerable to pilferage.
2. Rearrange the merchandise in vulnerable areas, if possible, or improve the lighting. Use of mirrors allows coverage of difficult areas from vantage points.
3. The most vulnerable days are, in order, Saturday, Friday, Thursday, Sunday, Monday, Wednesday and Tuesday. Most critical hours are reported to be 3 p.m. to 7 p.m. Attempt to have as much coverage as possible during these critical hours and on the more vulnerable days.
4. Offer rewards to store personnel for the detection of shoplifters.
5. Train all personnel in the techniques of detecting shoplifters.
6. Train all personnel in the procedure to be used after detection.
7. Be certain that every employee understands who is responsible for the apprehension of shoplifters. Don't allow sales personnel to become self-styled policemen. Don't invite a civil suit.
8. Work with local police and learn how they would like to help you handle the problem.
9. Duplicate simple instructions for all floor personnel and post them behind each counter.
10. After you have given all personnel adequate instruction in preventing shoplifting, don't feel you have conquered the problem and need not continually refresh their memories. Keep after this problem at regular intervals and make prevention of shoplifting a constant goal.

Suggestions for Store Personnel

1. Wait on all customers promptly.
2. Avoid turning your back to the customer.
3. Never leave your section unattended.
4. Be especially alert when groups of juveniles enter the store.

5. Prevent children from loitering and handling merchandise.
6. Observe closely people with baby carriages.
7. Observe closely people carrying large handbags, shopping bags, umbrellas and folded newspapers.
8. Be alert to people who carry merchandise from one location to another.
9. Don't allow merchandise to lie around the counter if it belongs somewhere else.

Shoplifter Concealment Techniques

1. Sometimes hair is rearranged to hide small items.
2. Palming is aided by use of packages and gloves.
3. Double elastic waistbands form hidden pockets inside skirts or trousers.
4. Professionals sometimes use rubber bands with a suction cup or hooks fastened inside a coat or jacket sleeve.
5. Slits often form false pockets in jackets, skirts, or trousers.
6. Umbrellas are a good catchall, especially when hung over the arm and held below counter level.
7. Wide skirts, capes and overcoats provide good hiding places.
8. A long belt with extra eyelets is often used to strap merchandise to the waist beneath outer garments.
9. Knitting bags, briefcases and newspapers form "pouches" for small-sized articles.
10. A rubber band around bundles of ties, stockings, socks, is used to hook items beneath outer garments.
11. Clothespin snappers, wire hooks or loops are fastened under arms, shirts or on round garters on the leg.
12. Hats, gloves, pocketbooks, and scarves are often worn out as the customer's own. Sweaters, too, can be worn or casually carried out.
13. Watch for the team that works the fitting room. One generally remains while the other moves repeatedly to the sales floor bringing new garments back and forth. In crowded conditions, they are able to hide or wear garments under their own clothing.
14. Watch sachels, boxes, large-sized purses which are carried into fitting or rest rooms.
15. Watch the hard-to-fit or hard-to-please woman who makes repeated trips to and from the fitting room. If rooms are not kept clear of surplus garments, it's impossible to keep an accurate check on the limited number she should have when she leaves.
16. Man-woman teams usually work this way: one serves as "lookout" while the other, in most cases, casually carrying a coat, lifts merchandise.

17. Entire bolts of piece goods can be stolen with relative ease by slick operators. They use special long-slit pockets built into coats.
18. A woman will sometimes tuck a sweater or blouse inside a jacket, then button it up and walk out.
19. A persistent bell-ringer in the self-service department may be distracting a clerk while an accomplice lifts merchandise.
20. Many articles are carried suspended between the legs. Men and women use garters and rubber bands to fasten stolen items to their calves.
21. Many shoplifters place a coat or jacket on top of the counter over the article they want. Then, it's simply a matter of picking up the coat and the item and walking out.

Point Checklist to Stop Profit Leaks

1. *Shoplifting:* Require all bags to be sealed. Don't stack merchandise on counters above eye level so supervisors and clerks see over a wide area.
2. *False Claims:* Employees should be instructed in observing and reporting accidents. The protective service should be called immediately.
3. *Theft and Pilferage:* Weak department controls encourage thefts. When possible, daily inventory is one answer. Fairly constant surveillance by department heads is a must. Keep more than one employee in each department at all times.
4. *Collusion Between Employees and Outsiders:* Switching price markers to favor a friend is a practice to look for. Spot check transactions at point of sales, after cash register has been rung up.
5. *Fraudulent Refunds:* Insist on approved sales slips, laxity in enforcing this procedure frequently results in losses.
6. *Damaging Merchandise to Render it Unsalable:* The offense may involve both sales people and receiving department employees. If loss becomes unusually heavy, investigation must be launched at places where damage is caused.
7. *Poor Check on Inventory:* Failure to get receipt when loaning merchandise from one department to another is gross carelessness. The answer is to make the rule ironclad—no interdepartmental transactions without proper record.
8. *After Hour Losses:* Could involve janitors and maintenance men, with or without outside confederates. Permit use of only one door for all employees; store guard to keep key in his possession. Check all admissions and departures.
9. *Losses in Transit:* Firm insistence on correct routine in transfer of merchandise from warehouse to store, or from store to store, makes it simple to check losses through shortage.

Summary

Initial contacts, corrective actions and disposition of employee or patron pilferers, when warranted, must be accomplished correctly to insure fair and just treatment of the suspect or accused and to protect the interest of the business. Inaccurate charges, insufficient or inconclusive evidence, procedural errors in operational and enforcement measures or in personnel actions to discharge employees for theft may only result in a miscarriage of justice or in undesirable retention or reinstatement of employee pilferers. Additionally, insufficient evidence or inaccurate charges and unwarranted or inconclusive actions damage the reputation and impair the morale of the suspect, whether he be employee or patron, and may have an unfavorable impact on other employees and patrons. And regardless of guilt, the sums awarded as punitive damages to the defendant in such cases can be astronomical.

Precise detailed rules, which are correct for every act of pilferage, cannot be established and followed by all facility and enforcement personnel. Guidance should be outlined to provide fair, orderly and legally permissible action and disposition in dealing with pilferers, suspected and known. Individual situations will vary with jurisdiction, operational requirements, and circumstances surrounding the pilferage, identity of pilferer(s) and ready availability of enforcement personnel.

Employee Action Against Pilferers

Certain courses of action must be prescribed for employees when they observe or suspect patron or employee pilferage. The following guidance is generally applicable and advisable at consumer outlets and storage facilities:

1. Observe suspects carefully but unobtrusively. Acts that appear to be thefts may in fact be carelessness, preoccupation, hurrying, or other natural and innocent traits on the part of honest patrons or employees.

2. When pilferage is reasonably suspected, the manager or other designated person(s) must be promptly notified. This may be done by another alerted employee, an activated signaling device such as a light, buzzer, or other expedient prearranged means.

3. Employees should discreetly keep suspects or pilferers in view without arousing their suspicion. This permits observance of hiding places for pilfered articles, other methods of operation, possible accomplices, and it aids in identifying pilfered items and pilferers.

4. Sales personnel and other such employees should not use force to detain pilferers. If their departure appears evident, the employee may approach and delay the pilferer in a conversation. Offers to help in item selection, wrapping, ringing up of items and like assistance may be used. In the event that designated personnel do not respond in time, all

employees aware of the theft should particularly note the pilferer's complete physical appearance, the time, items taken, description of transportation, direction of travel, associates, and other pertinent data. This information may be of assistance in subsequent apprehension or upon the pilferer's departure from the installation.

5. Pilferage by employees in consumer outlets, storage facilities or in transit does not generally require the same urgency as does patron pilferage. Prompt reporting and discretion are still required, but more detailed and informative reporting, verbal or written, is possible here. Particular attention should be given to identities or descriptions, location, time, quantities and types of items, methods of operation, associates, and transportation, including license numbers, direction of travel, and ideally, destination.

Supervisor-designated personnel who detect pilferage or are alerted to it by others generally have more latitude in such situations than do subordinate employees. Many of the same guidelines on observation, premature actions, and noting relevant information apply. Guidance described below may generally be followed. The pilferer's sex and age, location, type and amount of items stolen, professionalism involved, number of pilferers (patron and/or employee), and other particulars determine the required actions.

1. Supervisors must respond quickly to reports that pilferage is occurring or has occurred. Conduct should be such that uninvolved patrons or employees are not needlessly alarmed or notified. Alertness in approaching the location may provide an estimate of the situation before actual contact with reporting personnel or pilferers.

2. If time permits, employees or other reporting personnel should be questioned by supervisory personnel to determine clearly what they observed and heard (as opposed to what they suspect). Continued observation of the pilferer(s) may be indicated to confirm or eliminate suspicions.

3. The amount of pilfered property, number of persons involved, sex, age, attitude, as well as other factors, will indicate if the immediate assistance of security personnel is required. In many instances persons who are detected in the act of pilferage will respond to polite but firm requests to proceed from the immediate area of theft to an office or other location and will voluntarily wait until enforcement personnel arrive. Embarrassing scenes or inflammatory actions should be avoided whenever possible, and opportunities for flight with or disposition of stolen items should be minimized. Physical force to restrain pilferers is seldom justified and may have expensive legal ramifications.

9

Physical Security Surveys and Inspections

Scope

A survey should be a complete reconnaissance, study, and analysis of an installation's property and operations, noting any and all physical security hazards or deficiencies. The person conducting the survey must be thoroughly familiar with all physical security protective measures so that any recommendations are appropriate and practicable, and in the interest of economy without sacrificing security. Recommendations should be consistent with existing conditions, such as the environment, mission, resources available and the actual need for remedial action.

Forms of Surveys

Surveys may be initial, supplemental, or follow-up surveys. Special surveys may be made as required. An initial survey is, as the title implies, the first survey of an installation made by the responsible surveying office. A supplemental survey is made when there is a change in an installation's organization, mission, or physical aspects which affect its physical security. The purpose of the follow-up survey is to insure that recommendations have been carried out.

So that the initial survey record may be kept current and accurate, the same general subjects and specific points of security interest developed in the initial survey should be reexamined in subsequent follow-up surveys. In many instances survey personnel will find that recommendations have not been carried out but that work orders have been submitted and/or validated. In such instances the original deficiency is still reported as a deficiency until it is permanently corrected. A check should be made to determine that such work orders have actually been submitted to the proper action agency, and do not represent simply "paper filing."

Special surveys may be required for specific purposes, such as the occupation of a new area of the installation; the abandonment of an occupied area; proposed construction; disasters which cause extensive damages; and similar situations. The scope of the special survey should be limited to what is necessary to accomplish the specific purpose, as directed by the commander.

Survey Personnel

Inspection personnel should be carefully selected, since their findings have important implications for the security program. Personnel conducting surveys must be well trained in physical security techniques. They should understand that the security problem is determined by the nature of the business activity or product manufactured or stored; the economic and political situation of the area; the potential danger to security; and the logistical support available. They should clearly understand that installations may vary as to requirements for protective measures. Some installations may require only a single type of protection; in others, certain internal areas may require special protection, such as segregation or compartmentalization, with a maximum of protection measures.

Arrangements should· also be made for technical and administrative personnel to accompany the survey team where necessary.

Preparation

Before conducting a physical security survey, several steps should be taken to provide an adequate and practical estimate of the security situation:

1. A preliminary contact should be made with appropriate personnel to arrange time and other details.
2. Previous surveys, if any reports are available, should be checked for background information and action taken on noted deficiencies.
3. Determine the reasons for the survey, and the type of survey required.
4. Team personnel should be familiar with the mission and history of the installation or intended use of the area, and with any changes in mission or area use since previous surveys were made.
5. Obtain installation floor and ground plans from the engineer's office. Check them especially for utility openings, false ceilings, and similar areas where buildings can be entered.

6. Review installation regulations and operating procedures.
7. Prepare a checklist for use as a guide in making the survey.

Making the Survey

A physical security survey is made to verify current data and to obtain new facts. It should be conducted not only when the installation is in operation but at other times as well, including hours of darkness. It should provide data for a true evaluation of existing hazards and the effectiveness of current protective measures.

The use of a survey team permits specialization by the members and develops expertise in evaluating the various facets of physical security. For example, one member may examine the employment and training of the security guard force while another surveys the perimeter barriers and the protective lighting system. Any expedient division of duties is recommended.

Minimum Standards of Security

Security standards as developed from this text, and appropriate adopted security regulations, should be useful as a guide in evaluating a physical security program. After considering the prescribed minimum security standards and the facts brought out by the physical security survey, a careful balance must be sought between what exists, what is desired, and what may be necessary under conditions of national emergency.

Deficiencies affecting the entire installation that are identifiable through physical security surveys include the following:

1. Indication that perimeter security is inadequate.
2. Evidence that any part of the installation is being used for unlawful or unauthorized practices.
3. Indication that fences or lights are needed.
4. Disclosure that control and check of persons entering or leaving the installation are inadequate.

Surveys of individual facilities should include, but are not limited to, inquiry into:

1. Procedures for indoctrinating personnel in the use of internal control procedures, and for making them aware of the necessity for vigilance to prevent loss of money and property.
2. Receiving, stock control, and storage procedures.
3. Procedures used for receiving, holding, and banking money.
4. Structural characteristics of the buildings housing the facility.
5. Adequacy of security guard personnel and the effectiveness and enforcement of their orders.

6. Procedures of storing and accounting for narcotics and sensitive medications.

Units on an installation may also be surveyed. Surveys may include inquiry into:

1. Supply and storage room security and procedures.
2. Adequacy and application of guard orders.
3. Safeguarding money and property.

Surveys of units and facilities may be expected to uncover information relative to weaknesses in the security of their buildings, with respect to:

1. Locking devices and key control.
2. Pass system, if appropriate.
3. The adequacy of bars and/or protective screening over windows, skylights, and similar openings.
4. The potential of unlawful entry through attics, boiler rooms, basements, air vents, and crawl spaces under buildings.
5. The need for, or adequacy of, existing intrusion-detection systems.
6. Improper storage.
7. Lack or inadequacy of inventories and audits.
8. Lack of supervision or control in the unit or activity.
9. Indications of changes or alterations in records.
10. Excessive amounts of items on hand and their accessibility to unauthorized persons.
11. The refusal or failure to spot check employee work habits; the lack of internal control measures to assure honesty or to detect dishonesty, because of a mistaken belief that to do so would be poor leadership by casting aspersion upon the honesty of assigned personnel.

Evaluation

An evaluation of physical security must consider the availability of materiel and personnel. There will rarely be as much money, equipment, and manpower for security as are desired. When this is understood, the challenge for making the best of what is available must be accepted. Based on the mission and the potential security threat, the degree of reasonable and necessary security must be determined. The survey will indicate under two categories the elements required for the accomplishment of the installation's mission.

The evaluation should also indicate any areas of excessive security or overprotection. For example, there may be guard posts which are no longer required, due to changes in a specific area. Such situations should be examined closely, and appropriate recommendations made with a view of savings in manpower, materiel, or funds which may be used to better advantage elsewhere. The evaluation should draw recommendations from three basic areas:

1. Security personnel—recommendations affecting security guard utilization or employment.
2. Administrative or operational measures—recommendations for administration or operational procedural changes.
3. Physical security measures—recommendations regarding physical security factors, fences, lights, alarms, etc.

Survey personnel should procure and attach as exhibits to survey reports such of the following as are required for management's understanding of listed deficiencies and recommendations:

1. A copy of the installation physical security plan.
2. Documentary material in the form of current SOP, regulations, forms, maps, etc., which corroborate and are pertinent to the facts and findings contained in the body of the report.
3. Samples of personnel, visitor, and/or vehicular identification media.
4. Meaningful photographs and sketches. If the deficiency cannot be explained adequately in the narrative, use a photograph or sketch with the deficiency marked on it so it can be readily identified by the reader of the report.
5. Such additional evidentiary material as is deemed essential to support the points made in the report.

Exhibits must be identified alphabetically and attached to the report in the order in which they are referred to in the narrative. An index of exhibits must be attached on a separate sheet of paper immediately following the body of the report. Exhibits submitted with the initial survey report need not be resubmitted unless there have been changes; then, if practicable, only the changes need be submitted as exhibits.

Physical Security Inspection Checklist—Narcotics and Controlled Substances

1. Does the location of the room area afford adequate protection?
2. Is the room/building that houses the narcotics of permanent construction?
3. Are bulk narcotics/controlled substances stored in a vault or similar protective storage?

4. Is there an authorized narcotics cabinet/chest (hospital ward)?

5. Is the vault/safe/cabinet kept securely locked when not in use?

6. Are responsible personnel in close vicinity to assure protection?

7. If narcotics are stored in a small moveable safe, or the like, is the safe adequately secured to a permanent part of the storage room or building?

8. Are procedures established to insure strict accountability and control of narcotics and controlled drugs?

9. Is a narcotic and controlled substance register maintained?

10. Does it contain narcotic and controlled substance inventory?

11. Does it contain a narcotic and controlled substance record?

12. Is the register maintained properly?

13. Is a separate record prepared for each drug or on each item containing alcohol?

14. Is a joint inventory taken by the responsible person going off duty and the person coming on duty?

15. Is the balance on hand recorded in the appropriate column by both responsible persons?

16. Is the register secured and available only to authorized personnel?

17. Is the box heading of each record completed in its entirety, i.e., ward number, date, correct name of the drug, accountable unit of measure, and balance on hand?

18. When a drug is dispensed, is the complete information recorded as to disposition, i.e., day, hour, patient's name, initial and last name of doctor who ordered the medication, etc.?

19. When a unit of a narcotic or controlled substance is accidently destroyed, damaged or contaminated, is the fact entered on the record?

20. When accountable drugs are issued to a ward, are entries made by the pharmacy representative on the appropriate form, i.e., the day, hour, amount of drugs, and new balance?

21. Are corrections of errors in the drug register in accord with current regulations?

22. Are monthly inventories and verification of records conducted by an outside, objective officer?

23. Have there been any reports of loss, theft, or drugs unaccounted for within the past 12 months?

24. Is an intrusion-detection device/system installed?

Physical Security Inspection Checklist—Finance and Accounting Office

1. Is the finance office adequately guarded?

2. Have adequate precautions been taken to prevent unauthorized entrance after duty hours?

3. Have security measures been coordinated with other security forces?

4. Is the finance office equipped with adequate facilities for the storing and safeguarding of public funds and documents?

5. Do the safeguards employed during normal operations preclude loss, substitution, or pilferage of funds and documents?

6. Are vaults or safes accessible at any time to unauthorized persons?

7. Are unauthorized persons excluded from the working areas of the office by means of a railing or counter?

8. Are money-exchanging windows situated so as to prevent unauthorized access to funds? (If not, explain on separate sheet.)

9. Are internal office procedures established to provide controls on all undelivered and returned checks?

10. Is there a central point for their receipt, holding, and final disposition, with responsibility therefore charged to a specific individual?

11. Is the cashier provided with a separate working space or properly enclosed cage or room with a window for paying and receiving?

12. Is a cash drawer with key lock, or a field or similar safe, provided for safeguarding funds and vouchers during temporary absence of the clerks?

13. If more than one person in the office has cash in his possession, is each person provided with a separate and secure receptacle for such monies?

14. Are receipts taken for all funds entrusted to the cashier and receipts given the cashier for all funds returned or valid vouchers accepted?

15. Is there a procedure for unannounced verification of cash on hand?

16. Do current records indicate that such verifications are being made on an unannounced basis at least once each quarter?

17. Is positive identification of the payee made prior to any cash payments?

18. Is the amount of cash entrusted to a cashier always kept within the limits of his bond?

19. Upon receipt of shipments of blank checks, are the cartons examined and the serial numbers checked?

20. Does the finance and accounting officer or his deputy inspect the blank checks in current use at the beginning and end of each day's business to see that no blank checks have been extracted?

21. Are cartons bearing evidence of tampering opened and checks counted individually?

22. Does the finance and accounting officer maintain a daily record of the number of checks released, written, and returned for safekeeping?

23. Are spoiled and voided checks properly safeguarded?

24. When checks are voided or spoiled, are they properly marked and reported?

25. Is the mailing and/or delivery of checks properly controlled to prevent loss?

26. Is the cashier furnished with a weapon? If so, is he qualified in the use of it?

27. Do cashiers supply a receipt for cash received for each day's business?

28. What personnel are authorized access to keys to the finance office?

29. Are keys to the locking devices of the meter and protection unit of check-signing machines kept in the custody of the finance and accounting officer at all times?

30. Are keys or combinations to the cashier's safe and cash drawer in the hands of any person other than the cashier?

31. Are locks replaced when keys are lost or stolen?

32. Has the cashier sealed one key and/or the combination to the safe in an envelope suitably marked so that its unauthorized opening may be detected?

33. Is this envelope secured in the safe of the finance and accounting officer?

34. Is the combination to the finance and accounting officer's vault or safe known only by such officer and his assistant?

35. Is a copy of such combination, sealed in an envelope and suitably marked so that its unauthorized opening may be detected, delivered to the installation commander for use in the event of an emergency?

36. Are procedures established to provide two disinterested persons to witness the opening of either the cashier's or finance and accounting officer's safe when those responsible persons are not present?

37. Is there a requirement that the witnesses execute an affidavit as to the contents of the safe at the time of opening?

38. When vaults or safes are opened, is the dial shielded so that the operation of the combination cannot be observed by others?

39. Are the combinations of vaults and safes changed at least every six months?

40. Are safe combinations changed when newly appointed finance officers or cashiers open or take over an account?

41. Is there a guard post established at, in or near, the finance office?

42. If no such guard is furnished, is one required?

43. If a guard is provided, are his orders adequate? Is he fully familiar with his orders? Describe his duties.

44. Is there a plan establishing security requirements for funds in transit?

45. Is an intrusion-detection device/system installed?

Physical Security Inspection Checklist—Retail Businesses

1. Does the manager, at the end of each business day, inspect the premises to insure that all windows, doors, safes, etc., have been closed and that no person is hidden in restrooms or elsewhere? Is an intrusion-detection device/system installed?

2. Are service entrances locked from the inside when not in use for authorized movements of merchandise?

3. Is a strong light kept burning over the safe during nonoperational periods?

4. Is this light visible from the outside? Explain.

5. Are patrons positively identified prior to the consummation of any purchase?

6. Does any portion of the arrangement of the activity lend itself to pilferage or shoplifting? Explain.

7. Are authorized personnel available to observe patrons as a deterrent to shoplifting? Explain.

8. Are all personnel concerned familiar with procedures in handling shoplifters?

9. Is there a tally-in or tally-out system, as appropriate, for checking supplies received or shipped against shipping documents?

10. Are there any shortages in high-value items such as cameras, watches, jewelry, etc.?

11. What action is taken when high-value, identifiable items are missing?

12. Do sales slips indicate serial numbers of items normally possessing same?

13. If not, is such recording practical?

14. Are critical or sensitive items such as watches, cameras, etc. stored in separate secured storage in stockrooms or other areas? Describe storage of such items.

15. Are any items of comparatively high value and sensitivity displayed in such a manner that they could be readily stolen with little chance of discovery? Describe.

16. Are issues of sensitive items to sales clerks for display and subsequent sale documented in any manner? Describe.

17. Are service doors under the security of responsible employees when opened?

18. Are unauthorized personnel permitted to enter the exchange storerooms or the kitchen serving area of the food facility?

19. When it is necessary for vendors, maintenance personnel, or other individuals not directly connected with the exchange activity to enter stock or store rooms, are they always accompanied by an exchange employee?

20. Are garbage and trash inspected before removal to assure that this garbage or trash is not being used as a means of removing merchandise or material without authorization?

21. Are employees required to check all personal packages or parcels with the manager?

22. Are employees required to check with the manager prior to leaving the store?

23. Are periodic shakedown inspections of employees, their parcels and/or personal possessions conducted prior to their departure from the premises?

24. Are female employees permitted to take their purses into the aisles?

25. Are employees required to enter and/or depart the activity through one door under the supervision of office personnel?

26. Are employees permitted to ring up their own purchases?

27. Are all sales recorded on cash registers?

28. If not, how are such sales controlled?

29. Are excessive quantities of money removed from cash registers during daily operations?

30. Are such funds immediately turned in to the cashier or branch manager?

31. Are amounts rung up on cash registers observable by the customer?

32. Are surprise cash counts conducted?
33. Are all cash register drawers equipped with operative locks and keys?
34. Are cash register drawers kept locked when unattended?
35. Are change funds from each cash register bagged and turned in to the branch manager at the close of each business day?
36. Are personnel desiring to cash checks, money orders, or traveler's checks required to produce identification prior to cashing such instruments?
37. Are postdated checks accepted?
38. Are cashiers cages, booths, and/or other enclosures enclosed and provided with locking devices to prevent access by persons other than the designated cashier?
39. If not, is it practicable to provide such enclosures? Explain.
40. If the activity safe(s) do not exceed 1,000 pounds in weight, are they secured to the premises by being imbedded in a heavy concrete bed or steel strapped or bolted to the floor beam?
41. Can the safe be seen from the outside of the building?
42. Is such positioning of the safe possible?
43. Have the combination(s) to the safe(s) been changed when employees having access retire or are reassigned?
44. Is adequate control maintained over items taken into fitting room?
45. Are excessive inventory shortages promptly investigated?
46. Are armed guards provided for transfer of large sums of money to and from the activity?
47. Are employees assigned lockers or provided other containers to secure their personal property?
48. Is a list of personnel known to cash fraudulent checks available to the check cashier?
49. Are controls adequate to assure that any proceeds from old tires, batteries, used oil, etc., left by customers buying new items revert to the exchange and not to employees?
50. Are cash funds restricted to the minimum consistent with needs?
51. Are petty cash funds maintained?
52. Is comingling of funds between salespersons permitted?
53. Are daily cash turn-ins counted in the presence of the salesperson?
54. Is adequate protection afforded the courier making bank deposits or change runs?

Physical Security Inspection Checklist—
Warehouse Activities

1. Is there a specific procedure in effect that assures strict accountability of all property? (On separate sheet, show value of last inventory.)

2. Are the records of this activity subjected to periodic audits?

3. Are sufficient and comprehensive physical inventories conducted?

4. Are inventories conducted by disinterested (objective) activity personnel?

5. Are fixed and real property accounted for?

6. Are stock record or bin cards maintained?

7. Are stock levels on these cards verifiable through records of incoming stock?

8. Are issues recorded on these cards indexed to specific requisitions? (Voucher Numbers)

9. Are inventories recorded on these cards?

10. Is there excessive use of reports or surveys?

11. Is there a specific and secure procedure for the receipt of incoming property?

12. Are there any weaknesses in the present system for the physical unloading and storage of merchandise?

13. Are delivery personnel required to produce a bill of lading or other listing of the delivery?

14. Is an accurate tally conducted prior to acceptance?

15. Are delivery records checked against requisitions or purchase orders?

16. Is acceptance of deliveries limited to specific personnel?

17. Are incoming shipments carefully checked for signs of pilferage, damage, etc.?

18. Are shipping and receiving platforms free of trash and are shipments neatly stacked for proper observation and counting?

19. Are unauthorized persons kept from storeroom/storage areas?

20. Is a current personnel access list maintained?

21. Are supplies adequately protected against pilferage?

22. Are adequate protective measures afforded open storage?

23. Is material in open storage properly stacked, placed within, away from, and parallel to perimeter barriers, to provide unobstructed view by patrol personnel?

24. Are adequate locker and "break area" facilities provided for employees?
25. Is there a secure place to keep broken cases of damaged merchandise to prevent pilferage?
26. Is there a secure room or container for the safekeeping of sensitive items?
27. Are employees permitted to carry packages in and out of work areas?
28. Are there provisions for parking privately-owned vehicles to insure that they are not parked in an area offering an opportunity to remove items from the building to the vehicle without being detected?
29. Are trash collectors permitted in the building? (Janitorial help.)
30. If so, are trash containers inspected to assure no supplies are secreted in the containers?
31. Is there a specific procedure in effect for the issue and/or shipping of property?
32. Are there any weaknesses in the present system for the physical issue or shipment of property?
33. Are receivers required to receipt for the goods?
34. Are signature cards used for all authorized receiptors?
35. When issues are made by shipment, is there a means to verify their arrival at the requesting facility?
36. Are shipments or deliveries receipted to the carrier or the person making the delivery?
37. Are adequate controls maintained over property prior to issue?
38. Is responsibility for items fixed?

Physical Security Inspection Checklist—General

1. Is perimeter of facility defined by a fence or other type physical barrier? (If possible, attach typical photograph for exhibit purposes.)
2. If a fence is utilized as the perimeter barrier, does it meet the minimum specifications for security fencing?
3. Is it of chain-link design?
4. Is it constructed of #1-gauge or heavier wire?
5. Is mesh opening no larger than two inches square?
6. Is selvage twisted and barbed at top and bottom?
7. Is bottom of fence within two inches of solid ground?

8. Is the top guard strung with barbed wire and angled outward and upward at 45° angle?

9. Are physical barriers at perimeter lines damaged or deteriorated?

10. If masonry wall is used, does it meet minimum specifications for security fencing?

11. Is wall at least seven feet high with a top guard similar to that required on a chain link fence, or at least eight feet high with broken glass set on edge and cemented to top surface?

12. If building walls, floors, and roofs form a part of the perimeter barrier, do they provide security at least equivalent to that provided by chain link fence?

13. Are all openings properly secured?

14. If a building forms a part of the perimeter barrier does it present a hazard at the point of juncture with the perimeter fence?

15. If so, is the fence height increased 100% at the point of juncture?

16. Are openings such as culverts, tunnels, manholes for sewers and utility access, and sidewalk elevators which permit access to the activity, properly secured?

17. Do the doors exceed the number required for safe and efficient operation?

18. Are doors constructed of sturdy material?

19. Are all entrances equipped with secure locking devices?

20. Are they always locked when not in active use?

21. Are hinge pins to all entrance doors spot welded or peened?

22. Are all ventilators or other possible means of entrance to the buildings covered with steel bars or adequate wire mesh?

23. Are all windows securely fastened from the inside?

24. Are all windows not accessible from the ground adequately secured?

25. Are all openings less than 18 feet above uncontrolled ground, roofs, ledges, etc., protected by steel bars or grill?

26. Are openings less than 14 feet directly or diagonally opposite uncontrolled windows in other walls, fire escapes, roofs, etc., protected by steel bars or grills?

27. Has a key control officer been appointed?

28. Are locks and keys to all buildings and entrances supervised and controlled by a key control officer?

29. Does the key control officer have overall authority and responsibility for issuance and replacement of locks and keys?

30. Are keys issued only to authorized personnel?
31. Are keys issued to other than activity personnel?
32. Is the removal of keys from the premises prohibited?
33. Are keys not in use secured in a locked, fireproof cabinet?
34. Are records maintained indicating buildings and/or entrances for which keys are issued?
35. Are records maintained indicating number and identification of keys issued?
36. Are records maintained indicating location and number of master keys?
37. Are records maintained indicating location and number of duplicate keys?
38. Are records maintained indicating issue and turn-in of keys?
39. Are records maintained indicating location of locks and keys held in reserve?
40. Is a current key control directive in effect?
41. Are locks changed immediately upon loss or theft of keys?
42. Are inventories conducted at least annually by the key control officer to insure compliance with directives?
43. If master keys are used, are they devoid of markings identifying them as such?
44. Are losses or thefts of keys promptly investigated by control personnel?
45. Must all requests for reproduction or duplication of keys be approved by the key control officer?
46. Are locks rotated within the activity at least semiannually?
47. Are locks on inactive gates and storage facilities under seal?
48. Are they checked periodically by guard personnel?
49. Where applicable, is manufacturer's serial number on combination locks obliterated?
50. Are measures in effect to prevent the unauthorized removal of locks on open cabinets, gates, or buildings?
51. Are safe(s) located within the building?
52. Are safe(s) adequately secured to prevent removal?
53. Is the safe in a position where it can be observed from the outside by a security guard?
54. Is an alarm system used? (Briefly describe detection device on separate sheet.)

55. Is it a local alarm system?
56. Is it a central station?
57. Is it a proprietary system?
58. Is it connected to the guard headquarters?
59. Is it connected directly to a headquarters outside the activity proper?
60. Is it a private protection service?
61. Is it civil police protection service?
62. Is there any inherent weakness in the system?
63. Is the system backed up by properly trained, alert guards?
64. Is the system tested prior to activation for nonoperational periods?
65. Is the alarm system inspected regularly?
66. Is the system tamper-resistant?
67. Is the system weatherproof?
68. Is an alternate or independent source of power available for use on the system in the event of power failure?
69. Is the emergency power source designed to cut in and operate automatically?
70. Is the alarm system properly maintained by trained personnel?
71. Are properly cleared personnel utilized in maintenance of alarm systems?
72. Are frequent tests conducted to determine the adequacy and promptness of response to alarm signals?
73. Are records kept of all alarm signals received, including time, date, location, action taken, and cause for alarm?
74. Is protective lighting provided during hours of darkness?
75. Does it provide adequate illumination for all sides of the facility?
76. Are there provisions for emergency or stand-by lighting?
77. Are repairs to lights and replacement of inoperative lamps effected immediately?
78. Is there an auxiliary power source?

10

Security Education

Any security program or system will prove ineffective unless it is supported by an effective security education program. Security personnel cannot accomplish their mission without the active interest and support of every person on the installation. Such interest and support can be secured only through a good security education program.

It is obvious, from a review of the security hazards, that such a program must approach security from a "total package" viewpoint. It must be concerned not only with physical security measures designed to prevent such purely criminal acts as pilferage, but, just as importantly, with measures designed to provide security of information and materiels.

It is also essential that the security education program include all pertinent aspects of a crime prevention program. Many aspects of this program have a direct personal application to all installation personnel, and to their individual and collective morale and welfare.

Objectives

The goal of a security education program is to acquaint all personnel with the reason for security measures and to insure their cooperation. The security officer should attempt to instill in all personnel a willingness to learn and comply with all security regulations, to prevent infractions and violations, to follow established procedures and methods, and to report violations or breaches of the security system promptly to the proper authorities.

Basic Requirements

Security consciousness is not an inherent state of mind. It must be acquired. Many people are naive and trusting, are inclined to accept things at their face value. Pleasing as these characteristics are, they are not conducive to vigilance or security consciousness. Structural and mechanical aids to security are valueless without the active support of all personnel. All personnel must be made aware of the constant threat of breaches of security and of their individual responsibility to detect and thwart them. A continuous and forceful education program provides the constant awareness that successful security demands. The minimum requirements of an effective program should include:

1. Mandatory indoctrination for all personnel at times of assignment or employment.

2. A continuous program presented to selected audiences, primarily supervisors and other key personnel, in timely and applicable topics to develop and foster a high degree of security consciousness.

Security Indoctrination and Education

All personnel must be given security indoctrination. The reading of printed security regulations is not sufficient to insure complete understanding. Indoctrination should consist of a general orientation on the need for (and the dangers to) security and the individual's responsibility in preventing infractions. It should include a discussion of those hazards common to all personnel, with emphasis on the dangers of loose talk and operational carelessness. It should define the general security measures in effect, such as the pass system, private vehicle control, and package inspection. The security indoctrination is an introduction to the subject as applied to the particular installation. Further instruction should be applicable to the individual's duty assignment.

The areas of purely physical security (perimeter security, gates and doors, locks and keys, personnel identification and control, and so forth) can be incorporated into the "total package" program, utilizing materials found in this manual, as appropriate to each installation and in coordination and conjunction with all other security materials discussed above.

Crime Prevention

All security education programs should include materials on the crime prevention programs designed to eliminate or neutralize factors that cause individuals to commit criminal acts.

A security education program provides an excellent means of disseminating crime prevention information, and of encouraging the active participation of all personnel in observing and reporting security deficiencies, violations, or hazards of any nature.

Continuing Security Education

After the indoctrination, continuing security education should be more directly related to an individual's duty, in order to create and maintain

Figure 14. The security manager's attitude and his approach to the job are often reflected in the caliber of security provided. Attention to detail, alertness to all hazards, thoroughness in planning, executing, and evaluating the security program, and efficiency in operations are the measure of good security leadership. The appearance of such qualities at the top tends to instill them in other members of the security force.

interest. For example, the same possible security infractions do not confront the executive as confront the laborer or truck driver. The basic indoctrination alone may suffice for personnel who have little or no everyday contact with classified or critical information or materiel; but plans and training personnel, technicians, and craftsmen require a higher degree of instruction. Supervisors and executives require still broader understanding of their security responsibilities. Segregation of personnel by the level of security education they require will usually conform to their general academic background and make it possible for the instructor to select a level of instruction best suited to the audience. Separate instruction programs for each group should present subject matter within the group's interest. Suggested groupings, and the general area of their security education, follow:

1. Security officers should receive instruction in the general security, reponsibilities of their positions, the physical aids available as safeguards, and the enforcement policies and procedures of the installation.

2. Technicians, craftsmen, and others having access to classified information or materiel should be instructed in explanations of the terms

chain of custody and *need to know,* in telephone security, and in destruction procedures.

3. All personnel whose normal duties do not require access to materiel should be reminded constantly of the dangers of unrestrained talk about the duties they perform or materiel they handle; or about the classified projects, information or materiel with which they become knowledgeable as a result of their duties.

Program of Instruction

The security officer is responsible for planning an effective program of instruction. Profitable use of the limited time normally available for such instuction demands a competent instructor. The security officer should give the more important portions of the instruction. Other competent instructors may be used for less important phases or for phases which concern their areas of expertise.

The program should be based on an evaluation of the total security posture of the installation. It should begin with an explanation of the program, its aims and objectives—the *Why?* Then, develop the necessary tools to reach those aims and objectives—the *What?* Next, delineate methods of education by which the program will be conducted through individual and group conferences and meetings, speeches, use of news media, posters, placards, leaflets, etc.—the *How?*

The program must provide for initial and refresher training. It must also provide for debriefing of appropriate personnel upon their reassignment, retirement, departure on leave, and at other appropriate times. Above all, stress the absolute requirement for the support of every individual, regardless of any security clearance he may or may not have, and regardless of his work assignment.

The program should include materials on any recent incidents of security deficiency or violation, and any areas of laxity or trends which have become apparent in the security posture of the installation.

Posters, Placards, Leaflets, and Films

The methods of modern commercial advertising leave no room for doubt as to the effectiveness of constant repetition of a message. Many private industries make use of posters, placards, and leaflets to enhance their security education program. But some thought must be given to their display to reap the maximum benefit.

Posters usually should be large, depict an eye-catching illustration, and contain a brief, pointed message. They must be designed to impart their message at a glance. They should be displayed in locations where the maximum number of people pass or congregate, such as at entrances, gates, at the head of corridors, or on lunchroom walls.

Placards are usually small, may or may not be illustrated, and carry a lengthy message. They are designed for use where attention is necessary and where people must normally stop or are expected to loiter and have time to read. Examples of possible display locations are bulletin boards, counters, telephone booths, and in the vicinity of vending machines.

When posters and placards are issued in series, the method of display is dictated by the individual situation. Where display space is limited, they may be used one at a time and changed at intervals. Where the operation is scattered over a large installation, the posters and placards may be rotated among all the locations. When some of the posters or placards are particularly appropriate to the installation or operation, they can be given special display and kept posted for longer than normal periods of time.

Leaflets or pamphlets are usually pocket-sized and may or may not be illustrated. They are given to each individual, frequently as an enclosure in a pay envelope, and contain a brief, pointed message.

Many excellent films, both military and commercial, are available for showing. All opportunities should be taken for the showing of such films, on appropriate topics, to both selected and general audiences. Audio-visual personnel on all installations can be of assistance in selection and procurement.

Scheduling and Testing

Frequent short periods of instruction are more effective than less frequent, long periods. The ideas contained in four, well-planned, weekly 15-minute classes are more readily absorbed than those contained in a one-hour lecture once a month, regardless of how well the latter is planned and delivered. Instruction that infringes on the free time of the audience is seldom well received. Short periods of instruction to selected groups are easier to schedule without disrupting the operation.

In any form of instruction, testing serves the dual purpose of keeping the audience alert and indicating the efficiency of the presentation and the total program. Tests do not necessarily involve written answers. In fact, skits and hypothetical situations tend to enliven the instruction. Audience participation in giving consequences or solutions of situations presented will accomplish the same results.

Index